PRAISE FOR

Everybody Wants to Change the World

I love everything Tony Campolo writes, but *Everybody Wants to Change the World* may be his most down-to-earth book ever. This book goes straight to the bottom line: practical things that you, your family, your circle of friends, your class or small group or faith community can do this afternoon, tomorrow morning, or for years to come. If you're sick of wasting time talking and complaining, prescribe this book now and start looking for one or three or ten ideas in it that you will actually put into practice. The world will turn a bit further in the right direction—and so will you.

Brian McLaren
Author/Activist (brianmclaren.net)

Everybody does want to change the world, but few of us know where to begin. Gordon and Tony have created here a recipe for holy mischief. Within it are the simple, sassy, delectable ingredients to transform the world so that it conforms to the norms of the kingdom of God . . . all the while remembering that the revolution begins inside of us and infects the world through little things done with great love. Get ready . . . God is preparing us for something very, very small—and it is the small things that change the world.

Shane Claiborne
Author, *The Irresistible Revolution*

Everybody Wants to Change The World is a deeply and delightfully disturbing book full of practical ideas that is grounded in the biblical call to engage with the needs of the world. I wholeheartedly commend this thoughtful new resource to those thousands of campus and church leaders who are longing to move beyond hype and rhetoric to make a real difference to the world in the name of Jesus—one person, one day and one step at a time.

Pete Greig
Author, *Red Moon Rising*
Convener, 24-7 Prayer International

Gordon Aeschliman and Tony Campolo have created a highly practical resource that is packed with tangible suggestions for how to make a difference. It is biblically rooted and loaded with lived experiences waiting to be implemented. For students, small groups and all people of faith and conscience, this is a clarion call to action.

CRAIG DETWEILER

DIRECTOR, REEL SPIRITUALITY, FULLER THEOLOGICAL SEMINARY
COAUTHOR, *A MATRIX OF MEANINGS: FINDING GOD IN POP CULTURE*

Everybody Wants to CHANGE THE WORLD

Tony Campolo
& Gordon Aeschliman

Regal

From Gospel Light
Ventura, California, U.S.A.

Published by Regal Books
From Gospel Light
Ventura, California, U.S.A.
Regal   Printed in the U.S.A.

Regal Books is a ministry of Gospel Light, a Christian publisher dedicated to serving the local church. We believe God's vision for Gospel Light is to provide church leaders with biblical, user-friendly materials that will help them evangelize, disciple and minister to children, youth and families. It is our prayer that this Regal book will help you discover biblical truth for your own life and help you meet the needs of others. May God richly bless you.

For a free catalog of resources from Regal Books/Gospel Light, please call your Christian supplier or contact us at 1-800-4-GOSPEL *or* www.regalbooks.com.

Cover design by Josh Talbot Design (www. joshuatalbotdesign.com)

The websites and resources listed are provided for informational purposes only and do not necessarily represent the views and opinions of the authors or the publisher.

Library of Congress Cataloging-in-Publication Data
Campolo, Anthony.
 Everybody wants to change the world / Tony Campolo and Gordon Aeschliman.
    p. cm.
 Includes bibliographical references.
 ISBN 0-8307-4283-2 (trade paper)
 1. Christian life. 2. Social service—Religious aspects—Christianity. 3. Voluntarism—Religious aspects—Christianity. 4. Social gospel. 5. Church work. 6. Church and social problems. I. Aeschliman, Gordon D., 1957- II. Title.
 BV4520.C28 2006
 261.8—dc22   2006021937

1   2   3   4   5   6   7   8   9   10   /   10   09   08   07   06

Rights for publishing this book in other languages are contracted by Gospel Light Worldwide, the international nonprofit ministry of Gospel Light. Gospel Light Worldwide also provides publishing and technical assistance to international publishers dedicated to producing Sunday School and Vacation Bible School curricula and books in the languages of the world. For additional information, visit www.gospellightworldwide.org; write to Gospel Light Worldwide, P.O. Box 3875, Ventura, CA 93006; or send an e-mail to info@gospellightworldwide.org.

Contents

Introduction

Each year, millions of Americans take to the streets in their communities to volunteer on behalf of others. From soup kitchens and dental clinics to tutoring and construction, people pack their weekends and vacations in their quest to make a difference in the world. And close to a half-million Americans go abroad annually to find ways to change the world.

Just about every idea on this earth has shades of the good, the bad and the ugly. The desire to change the world is no exception.

There are some patently ugly ways to change the world. Flying an airplane into an office building would be an idea that most of us agree sits in the ugly column, as does dropping bombs on a village or city. Violence destroys the world, and yet that is how we often go about changing the world. What a strange approach—and what a common story. All too often, we are so convinced of the "rightness" of our idea that we willingly use force and destruction to impose that idea on others. Our very actions invalidate our mission.

Often, little about our outreach has anything to do with honoring the local community, serving their interests, or fitting into their ideas of what makes sense for their country. We've all heard the term "ugly American," a label we usually earn through our subtle but highly unattractive ways of changing the world. Many cultures around the world experience the onslaught of American volunteers as an invasion. We are often viewed as loudmouthed, aggressive, demanding, arrogant and spoiled. In our excitement to make a difference in the world, we can easily trample others or offend native peoples with our superior sense of what the world needs. Sometimes, it seems as if we are meeting our own needs (wanting to feel good about what we do) rather than truly serving others.

Everybody Wants to Change the World is the fruit of our travels to all 50 states in this country and to more than 100 countries around the globe. In our travels, we have been inspired by the lives of those who seem to have so little compared to the wealthy in the West—women and men living on less than a dollar a day. These folks model a deep, sacrificial love on behalf of people who have less than they do—the poor giving to the poor. These are the people we can learn from, because they understand how to meet the needs of others in loving, effective ways.

It's tempting to want to travel halfway around the world to "fix" the problems of poverty we see. Yet money or a little volunteer labor is not the real answer. Why? Because the world experiences material poverty for a number of reasons. The truth is, more often than not, people are made poor because of oppression. The political and economic systems of this world do not benefit the poorest of the poor. In fact, the rule of thumb would appear to be that the systems that make the wealthy more wealthy make the poor more poor at the same time.

When we rush around to help poor people in the world improve their lives, too often we are simply putting salve on a wound created by our own wealth. When we tend only the surface needs of the poor, it is as if we are simply building better houses for slaves. We feel like we have done something beneficial for humankind, but all we have done is make people a little more secure in their poverty or oppression.

We'd like to challenge your notions of how to best change the world. We think that changing the world has as much to do with the renewing of our own hearts and minds as it does with doing something practical "out there." And we believe that all of our encounters with the poor are opportunities for our lives to become transformed by their wealth of spirit and their wisdom.

We hope this resource will be a handbook for positive change. Although we have written primarily with college students and church youth groups in mind (because they tend to have the most fervor about changing the world), it is our hope that this action guide will be useful for many others as well. We believe that we have put together a package that can be useful for an afternoon or a lifetime.

Our ideas fall into several different categories and contain projects that can be done over a weekend, a spring break, a summer or a lifetime. The ideas can be implemented at a computer screen, in our local communities, and across the ocean. What we are suggesting ranges from direct encounters to study opportunities abroad, giving money to important causes, holding the public accountable for its treatment of others, or being downright creative. We have selected dozens of organizations that we think are good portals for entering the world. Each of the organizations offers further steps for really great ways to make a difference.

The adventure of changing the world is a journey that begins with our inner transformation. We hope this resource serves as a welcome invitation to you to travel that demanding road.

Yours for the world,

Tony Campolo
and Gordon Aeschliman

Poverty

CARING FOR THE POOR

When Jesus walked the earth, He demonstrated a special love and concern for those who were disadvantaged and pressed down by the harsh realities of living. He had compassion for the underprivileged and deprived. "I tell you the truth, whatever you did for one of the least of these brothers of mine, you did for me" (Matt. 25:40).

Jesus never approached the poor as some kind of project or problem that had to be rectified. He genuinely felt the weight of their plight. This should not surprise us, because in the Old Testament, God regularly measured Israel's faithfulness by the degree to which they cared for the poor. To ignore the poor was a direct offense against Yahweh.

There have been times in the past when our society was confused about our responsibility to the poor. Even our spiritual leaders seemed to get this mixed up from time to time. "Evangelism is the great and singular priority," some would say. The fear was that if Christians became too involved in the physical dimension, they might lose their spiritual orientation and forsake the evangelism mandate. They would be too busy feeding mouths to feed souls.

This temporary departure from the full call of the Scriptures is an unfortunate blip on the screen of the modern Church. We do not have permission to forsake any dimension of our calling—including caring for the poor. Indeed, the Church hurt its witness by inviting the criticism that Christianity has no earthly value. People would say, "Christians do nothing to make the earth a better place; they're only concerned about what lies beyond this life." Unfortunately, many times, such critics were right. That form of Christianity—which ignores the immediate needs of our fellow man—has no value to the world. Besides, that line of thinking certainly is not biblical.

Thank God those days are largely behind us. Yes, a few groups are still holding out for a truncated version of the gospel, but they do not reflect the spirit of the larger Church. The gospel is indeed good news for the poor, and we can preach the evangelistic message with integrity because we know that the Lord of our souls looks compassionately upon our physical suffering as well. If a child asks an earthly parent for bread, he or she will not be given a stone (see Matt. 7:9-11). How much more can we expect from our perfect heavenly Parent?

Who are the poor today? They are the hungry, homeless, unemployed and impoverished. They are always living on the verge of destruction. A single negative event added to their current burdensome plight can render them absolutely desolate. We see them on our TV screens—literally millions of men, women and children in Africa just days away from death by starvation. We see them in countries torn by wars—victims of conflicts they did not create nor desire, homeless and without adequate medical attention for their wounds. We see them in the rural communities and urban centers of America—unemployed, malnourished, uneducated and unable to get medical care. More than 1.2 billion people throughout the world may be living on the edge of death as a result of the impoverished conditions in which they live.[1] That is approximately 1 out of every 5 human beings.[2]

Clearly, Christians who love and obey Jesus are stirred by these facts. They do not cling to their wealth and attempt to justify their lifestyles. Rather, they ask, "What can I do?" And this question does not spring from a superior attitude that denigrates those who live in poverty. These Christians understand that it is the Lord who gives them breath to live and that He has provided them all the other gifts. They realize, "There but for the grace of God go I."

Caring for the poor, then, is not some kind of charity we dispense at a distance. No, as followers of Christ, we feel the pain of the poor intensely. We cannot live separate from their dilemma any more than we can ignore the pain of our own brother or sister.

Caring for the poor requires looking for long-term solutions that will provide lasting relief for people's impoverished circumstances while attempting to alleviate their immediate pain. It means reaching out to give a helping hand to people just like us—our *equals* who have not experienced the bounty that we have been graced to receive. It means putting aside our prejudices toward the poor and homeless and receiving them into our lives in the same way the King of heaven has received us.

The world cannot argue with a Church that lives in the pain of society's poor. The integrity of this form of Christianity silences the harshest of critics, because they know genuine love and compassion when they see it. And the truth is, they want it.

Project 1: Soup's Up

Soup kitchens are as old as urbanization. In large population centers there have always been and always will be just too many cracks through which people can fall. Jobs are lost, family support structures fail, folks are evicted from their apartments, and a spiral of demeaning poverty quickly ensues. Try to wrap your mind around this: In New York City alone, there are more than 1,200 soup kitchens that work together in a coalition to serve more than 1 million people every week.[3]

One of the more inspiring stories is of a group of moms who live on less than a dollar a day in South Africa. These moms could not afford to send their children to public school because the cost of books and transportation was out of reach. However, with the help of a small loan, these moms were able to band together to start a community vegetable garden. They opened a café in one of their homes and offered a creative menu based on what they raised. But from the very start, they also committed to providing free soup to anyone in their community who was HIV positive or too poor to afford proper nutrition. (Some HIV medicines have to be taken in conjunction with food.)

It's always inspiring how the poor find ways to provide for people who have nothing. Sometimes, it feels like an indictment against us in the wealthy West, who are always throwing away food because we have too much—and yet the hungry live right among us as well.

As you lay the foundation for opening a soup kitchen, your first priority should be to build a team of coworkers who can make a commitment to work a regular schedule for a set period of time (six months, one year, and so on). Then make a start by setting up a Saturday or Sunday evening soup kitchen in a local community building that has approved public cooking facilities (such as a church or synagogue). Give it an upbeat name, such as "Café Paris." Create the space in such a way that communicates warmth and fun and lets people know that they are welcome. The atmosphere could be enhanced with candles and live music (name two college students who don't want a chance to perform live!).

Set a menu that is simple, yet delicious. It's important to avoid the idea that those without food will do fine on a boring sandwich. Tap in to local resources and consult a chef or restaurant owner to find out how to create four or five sandwich and soup combinations that are healthy, filling and visually appealing.

Given the fact that your workforce is made up of volunteers and your rent is free, your newly launched Café Paris can be funded by a very small base of paying clientele. Write up a price board for paying customers, and make sure to invite local youth groups and all your relatives living in the region to come out and financially support the effort.

To ensure the dignity of those who cannot afford to pay, create a coupon that offers a free soup and sandwich. Distribute these coupons directly to patrons in your community who would benefit from the café, or leave them at your local social services office. You might also consider setting up a resource table in the café. This table could have information on public services in town that provide a variety of social needs. If you know a credentialed social services person who is interested in the soup-kitchen venture, she or he could personally host the table.

For information on how the New York City Coalition Against Hunger runs its soup kitchens, visit its website at www.nyccah.org.

Project 2: Local Food Drive

Shelters and soup kitchens have to find a massive amount of food every day to supply their pantries and fridges. Yet there is a very simple way to help these organizations with their food needs.

Here's how it works: Contact two or three local organizations that provide a food service to the hungry in your town. Ask them what kinds of food items they would like to have stocked on their shelves regularly (you will want to focus just on the nonperishable items such as canned soups, sugar or canned vegetables). Put together a simple shopping bag made of canvas that has a community statement on the one side (for example, "Shoppers Against Hunger in Peoria"), and then, on the other side of the bag, print the logos of several businesses in town that have agreed to join the effort (this is how you cover the cost of producing the canvas shopping bags—the businesses pay to have their name printed on the bag).

Next, print out a short list of items that someone could pick up while doing his or her regular weekly shopping. Make it really doable—three cans of soup, two cans of vegetables, two cans of fruit. Try to figure out items that would cost between $5 and $15. Put the list in the bag.

Approach several grocery stores in town and ask if you can set up shop outside their stores each Saturday morning (or whatever time works for your team of hunger activists). Post a sign at your table that will catch the attention of local shoppers. Ask folks to pick up a canvas bag when they enter the shop and to fill it with the items that are listed inside. Explain that any amount they purchase will help—whether it is one, two or all of the items listed in the bag.

When the shoppers come outside, they can simply drop the bag off at the table (remember, the bags are reusable). Offer each shopper a little thank-you sticker or pin that has your logo on it, and invite people to drop by each time they come shopping. You will be surprised to find out how many people like to add this act of kindness to their regular shopping routines.

Arrange with the shelters or soup kitchens to have their staff come and pick up the food at the end of each gathering-in day. Also, ask these organizations to provide you with a little informational display for your table so that local folks can learn about the variety of shelters or soup kitchens you are supplying.

This is a win-win situation. Local shelters get a good supply of staples, shoppers get that "feel good" sensation every time they are at the grocery store, and the local stores get more sales. You will even find that some grocery stores will agree to supply some of the food at a discount or that they will agree to match part of your donors' purchase totals.

Project 3: Donate Your Room

You've probably seen the overflowing dumpsters at the end of the semester at your college or university. Unbelievable! Who would have guessed that couches, TVs, microwaves, computers, entire wardrobes and beds could be trashed with such ease! Even if you haven't seen college campus dumpsters, chances are you've seen perfectly good things trashed in your own neighborhood or city.

Across America, in about the space of two weeks, a couple million students throw away enough furnishings to fund scores of organizations that work for the poor. This seems like an incredible waste. Why not collect these items and donate them to local thrift stores?

There are two primary systems that thrift stores use to distribute provisions to the poor. The first system is to simply make a large number of used wares available to the poor at a very low cost: shirts for $1, a winter jacket for $5, a couch for $10, a dinning room table or small TV for $15. For hundreds of thousands of Americans, thrift stores are the difference between an empty apartment and a minimally furnished home. For some, it is the only means by which they can obtain warm clothing to protect themselves from the cold December air.

The second system is to provide secondhand items to a slightly less-poor community while also raising funds for the poor. The thrift stores that employ this strategy are typically owned and operated by organizations that do community development work on behalf of the poor. A shirt at these stores might cost $3 instead of $1, but the idea is to keep the prices low enough so that nearly everything that is shipped in each week is sold. Because these stores have very low overhead (most staff donate their time, and the stores do not have to pay for large warehousing), the money from each day's sales goes directly to outreach programs for the poor. This system is effective as long as the prices are kept low enough to keep the merchandise moving and as long as there is a regular supply of used materials coming through the back door.

At the end of the school year (or whenever you find that you're not going to use some of your things), why not offer up some of your things as a bonanza to these kinds of organizations? Start by connecting with the various thrift stores in town. Find out if they are prepared to receive a massive shipment of used goods at one time. Work with universities in your area to come up with a way of collecting all the goods from the students as they move out en masse.

Some students have used the following approach: Using yellow tape, they marked off a large area near each major dormitory so that students could drop off their goods for donation rather than hauling them to the dumpster. The university allowed the students to hold donated dorm materials in these areas for 24 hours and gave the students permission to operate university vehicles to haul the goods to the various thrift stores in town. Another method is to arrange for the thrift stores to send their truck to pick up all the goods from designated locations. In one town, seven different thrift stores had their own dorm pile of goods ready for pickup!

This effort may take a day or two out of your life (and your friends'), but it is a very simple way to ensure that what could be the bed, kitchen table or couch for a poor family doesn't become a meaningless piece of junk in the local landfill.

Project 4: Planned Famine

By some estimates, as many as 40,000 people die of poverty-related circumstances every day.[4] As many as 6 million children die every year from hunger.[5] And, astonishingly, in the United States, 13 million children are considered to be living in hunger.[6]

A planned famine is a really great two-day event for people who want to learn more about the plight of the hungry world while also feeling a bit of what that means. It's also a good way to get different kinds of groups to cooperate with each other—for example, a couple of student groups on campus that focus on poverty and social justice, or three different religious campus groups that don't normally work together. Sometimes it takes focusing on the world outside of ourselves to realize that those closest to us are also sacred human beings, whether or not we agree with their beliefs.

A planned famine is typically a 30-hour program that begins at 6 P.M. on a Friday or Saturday night and runs until midnight the next day. The entire 30 hours are packed with games, multimedia presentations about the hungry, and group discussions about hunger. No food is eaten during the entire 30-hour period, although all kinds of juices and water are usually made available. At midnight, once the 30 hours are over, everyone goes out to a café together for their closing event—food.

You need to locate a building where you can have a lockdown for the 30 hours. (Often, a local church, synagogue or mosque will donate the space for the event.) Participants bring along a sleeping bag and pillow, a notebook, pens and pencils, favorite card games and, hopefully, a toothbrush and toothpaste as well.

Everyone agrees to leave the snacks at home or back in the dorm.

Construct the program so that there is some rhythm and breathing space for fun and organized learning. As facilitators, bring along a variety of supplies and resources for the participants. You'll need large newsprint, art supplies, educational materials and games. We recommend that you connect with the Bread for the World Institute (www.bread.org/about-us/institute/) for a number of helpful resources to use over the weekend. They can help you with videos, posters, statistics, games and more.

Plan some get-to-know-you games at the beginning of the 30 hours. Find out something interesting about everyone who came and learn why each person decided to attend the event. Then divide people up into small groups and have them make up a poster board about what they know about the hungry world. Have each group hang their poster and describe it to the rest of the group. Next, gather everyone back together again to watch a good video or DVD that has educational content about the epidemic of hunger. Have the group discuss what they learned from the video. After that, begin an informal set of games for fun. Be sure to have lots of great music on hand as well. Then it's lights out at 2 A.M.

Wake everyone by 10 A.M. to begin the next day's activities. For your three "meals" during this day, have everyone sit down around tables that are set with plates, silverware, serving bowls and baskets. But instead of food, only serve water and juice. Inside each serving bowl, have some prepared bits of information about world hunger. These could be statistics, stories or dilemmas that you found at the Bread for the World website or from other sources.

At each table, have people pass around the serving bowls as they serve up a portion of "hunger" for their meal. It's a great, symbolic way of connecting to hunger. Then have each person read what his or her serving teaches about hunger. Go around the circle until everyone has had a chance to share his or her information. If you have several tables, each group can have the same set of hunger servings. Formally end each meal with some kind of symbolic act—lighting a candle, silence or prayers.

Between meals, plan a good mix of games to play, videos to watch and study packets to go through as small groups during formal break times. Be sure to talk out loud about how hunger is affecting members of the group. Are their emotions on the rise? Are they finding themselves easily irritated? Do they feel tired and unmotivated? Are they experiencing any pain in their body?

For your last group event before the 30 hours is up, have your original small groups make up new posters on what they believe people can do about the hungry world. Have the groups display the posters around the room and then talk about them. Offer enough quiet space at the end so that everyone can make personal commitments to do something about the hungry. End the event at midnight by having everyone go out together for a thankful meal.

Project 5: Plug the Debt

One of the greatest causes of poverty in the world today may be the consequence of lending practices by European, American and Japanese banks to countries that are emerging from years of colonial rule.

On the surface, it sounds strange to say that the wealthy have made the world poor, especially if we consider that the wealthy of the world are the largest source of kindness to the poor. However, the sad fact is that developing countries have become so strapped with the burden of repaying debts to the West that they are not able to address their own social problems on even a minute scale. Today, the poorest countries in the world spend more money on the interest of their debt payments than they do on their total national budgets for health care and education for children. Money literally pours from the homes of the poor into the hands of the wealthy. And there is no way out of this mess unless we see a change of heart from those in the West.

Here's how this debt problem emerged. In the 1960s and 1970s, when the Cold War was at its height, Western banks loaned billions of dollars to impoverished young nations. The idea was to attract the poor away from the lure of Communism, a system that promised to side with the poor instead of the wealthy West. Western economists and social engineers were sent to these poor nations to show the leaders how the "religion" of the West—a free-market economy—would bring about a harvest of wealth for all.

To jump-start the system, the generous West would provide the loans. Of course, these loans went into building massive energy and agriculture systems that were then outsourced to companies from the West. The loans, in the short run, filled the coffers of Western corporations instead of companies in the poor nations.

The optimistic projections of the West never came to fruition, and by the end of the Cold War, billions of dollars were owed to Western nations. The debt was structured to greatly benefit the wealthy and, as a consequence, some countries have already paid back more than three or four times the amount they originally borrowed. Yet they have only paid interest—the entire principal is still owed.

We believe that the poorest nations must be forgiven this debt to the West. To do otherwise would be to literally enslave the future generation of the world's poor to work in perpetuity for banks owned by the wealthy. Children yet to be born will not have access to safe drinking water, immunizations, education or homes because their grandparents were burdened with repaying these loans.

So what can you do? One idea is to join a movement that has spread throughout the world known as "Jubilee." Named after a biblical notion that the land should be returned to its original owners after 49 years of use by another (see Lev. 25), Jubilee seeks to see the entire debt load of the poorest nations forgiven. To join the U.S. branch of Jubilee aimed at ending economic slavery, go to their website at www.jubileeusa.org.

Project 6: Slow Down to a Dollar

The statistics on poverty in the world are almost too large for us to grasp: 1.2 billion people live on less than one dollar a day; 2.8 billion people live on less than two dollars a day.[7] Clearly, for these people life has no margins and no quick fixes.

It may be a moral issue for those of us with means that we are able to go through our days without giving much thought to people who live with so little. But perhaps it is because those numbers are so staggering. In fact, some suggest that we suffer from compassion fatigue—the feeling that we have already done so much for poverty that we become exhausted at the thought of one more starving child, one more natural disaster, one more refugee camp created through war.

Yet to push aside half the world's population from our minds is another kind of poverty—a poverty of our spirits. Can we really afford to become entirely shut off to the sad fate of half of humanity and live as though they don't really matter? In the confusion over what to do about so large a challenge, we can easily slip into becoming completely insulated from their reality.

One simple idea for combating this compassion fatigue is to try to live on less than one dollar a day once per month. Commit to doing this for a year with a group of friends who also want to go on the same spiritual journey of keeping the poor alive in their hearts. After the year is up, evaluate how the discipline has shaped your lifestyle and commitments regarding the needs of the poor.

Living on less than one dollar will be a challenge, because you will have to deprive your body for 24 hours. You will probably have to fast for the day—or at the most eat a can of soup that you purchased for less than one dollar. Your beverages will consist of water from the faucet. And you won't be able to drive very far, because you'd probably use up one dollar worth of fuel in just a few miles.

If you want to turn this into a truly honest exercise, limit the time your lights are on, the time your heater or air conditioner is working, the time your TV is running and the time your computer is powered on. Doing so will leave you with some free hours, so plan to take a long walk, read a book in the library, or spend the evening with friends on a candlelit patio trading stories about ways to make a difference with your life.

Slowing down to a dollar a day will put your fast-paced lifestyle on hold and will offer you the chance to not only reflect on the immensity of global poverty but also get personal about it. When you are deprived of your normal routines and feel the discomfort of not having enough food, you will have placed poverty at the center of your life.

Project 7: Give a Dollar a Day

Those who are among the 1.2 billion people forced to live on less than one dollar a day must depend on nonfinancial resources to get through life. For these individuals, the two most important lifelines are their social networks (family, medical services, education systems) and their environment.

Over 80 percent of people who live on less than one dollar a day live on small plots of land, where they try to eke out their living through farming and raising chickens. There is a saying that holds true for these folks: To hurt the earth is to hurt the poor. Almost a billion people depend on the health of the earth every day to ensure their own personal health. And more than 300 million people depend on healthy forests, clean water, biodiversity and the shelter of tropical cover to ensure their future.

At the bottom of the pile—to put it crudely—live poor women and children. They always lose when the earth is devastated by storms, earthquakes and landgrabs. But perhaps the untold story is that they most often lose their land to large agricultural firms that buy up the fertile valleys and to factories that pour pollutants into the rivers that normally water the crops. It is not uncommon for the poor to bear the brunt of environmental toxins in the United States as well—fully 85 percent of all toxic sites in the nation are located in communities of poverty.

An organization called Target Earth focuses on the poor of the earth. Their slogan is simple enough: "Serving the Earth, Serv-ing the Poor." Their longer mission reads: "Serving the Earth and the poor in regions of the world where people live on less than a dollar a day." Target Earth looks for villages and communities that have been bypassed by the large development companies and seeks to identify local, indigenous solutions to environmental poverty.

The work of Target Earth is funded by a simple mechanism: People give one dollar a day to help the organization serve people who live on one dollar a day. There's something both symbolic and material about this approach. Sending away a check every month for one dollar a day reminds people who are wealthy that they really do have a lot of resources. Looking for ways to cut one dollar out of their daily budget becomes a highly spiritual act of service—and a reminder that they need to serve others who have to make it all work on just one dollar. And of course, the one dollar they give each day funds actual programs that care for the earth and those who depend on the earth for their future. Figure out how to cut one dollar a day out of your budget and then send the funds off to Target Earth. Make it at least a one-year commitment. And pull your friends or club members into the same effort. Make a goal of finding a dozen people on your campus who will stay committed to helping the poor of the earth for one year. Pool your funds each month and send them off to make a real difference.

You can contact Target Earth at www.targetearth.org.

Project 8: Hunger Banquet

Most of us are happy to be invited to a banquet. Not all banquets, however, are equal . . .

One of the images of wealth is a fancy ballroom event accessible only to people of means or status. Political fund-raisers, businesses wooing clients, famous people rallying support for a cause—these events become a fashion parade of the beautiful and the successful. Tabloids run the stories about these dazzling affairs and TV shows feed the bizarre fascination we have with those who seem to be more important than ourselves.

Food functions as a gathering point for societies. Yet isn't it a bit obscene when the food is lavishly spread in front of those who really don't need it or care to eat it? For those who are hungry, food is sacred. It is about their very survival and the future of their families.

Haven't we all heard college students complain about their cafeteria food? "There's nothing to eat!" they exclaim, which is a truly amazing statement when we consider the vast array of options of food available to them. When we consider the fact that a large percentage of the world goes to bed hungry every night, this is truly an embarrassing mind-set that we all have.

We suggest that you throw a hunger banquet on your campus or at your religious center. Here's how it works: First, decide what size group you can accommodate for dinner. Then, advertise a Global Banquet and send invitations to your student body or congregation. Charge $10 per person to attend the event.

Next, divide up your guest list according to world percentages on wealth and hunger. For example, if you decide to invite 100 participants, 45 of them would be from the world of extreme poverty, 20 would be poor, 20 would be adequate, 12 would be wealthy, and 3 would be extremely wealthy. Place each person's currency for the evening's meal in an envelope marked "Group A," "Group B," "Group C" and so forth to designate his or her group. Hand this envelope to each guest as he or she arrives.

As you plan your event, be sure that you have two large rooms available for the evening's festivities. Designate the first room to be a kind of waiting area. Hang art or exciting posters from around the world and have ethnic music playing in the background. The idea is to create an upbeat atmosphere. The second room (closed off to the first) will be the actual banquet hall. Have the food in the banquet hall set up buffet style. Put a price tag on each food item and on the plates, silverware, glasses and napkins. The fare should range from rice to steaks to salads and vegetables and include an array of drinks and deserts.

Once all the guests have arrived, welcome them to the Global Banquet and invite those in Group A to go first. As the people in this group enter the banquet room and survey the buffet, explain that they have currency in their envelopes to purchase whatever items they want for dinner. Tell them that you have put enough currency in their envelopes to allow them to eat anything on display and have all the utensils they require. They won't have to budget or choose which items they can afford.

Once the people in Group A have their food, seat them at a table that you have spread with an expensive tablecloth and flowers. Once they have started eating, fetch Group B. The people in this group will have less currency in their envelopes and should be seated at a table that is more plainly set than the first group. Once they begin eating, invite in Group C, then Group D, and so forth. By the time you get to the final group representing the 45 percent of the world that exists in extreme poverty, they will only have enough currency to purchase some rice and water. In fact, they will have to share paper plates, because they won't have enough money for each person to buy a plate *and* his or her simple dinner. Instead of seating them at a table, have them sit on the floor. Once they have started eating, project a 30-minute presentation on world hunger on the wall next to them.

We've hosted this event several times and have always found it to be a thought-provoking way of inviting people into the question and experience of world hunger. Every banquet has its own unique outcome. Sometimes the wealthy group starts to share its food with the poor. Sometimes they are just oblivious or assume something went "wrong" with the planning, because some people ended up on the floor with only rice. Sometimes the poor beg or steal from the wealthy.

What can make this banquet particularly effective is to have a facilitator with strong group skills host a discussion at the end. At one of the events we hosted, a pregnant mom came to the banquet. For this particular event, we had encouraged people to eat nothing all day before the banquet. (The idea was to make them more in touch with their feelings of hunger and panic if they were part of the poorest group). The pregnant mom, who was placed in the last group, was nearly beside herself as she described the strain of being hungry all day and then again that night while wanting to take care of the child in her womb.

Sometimes participants are angry, sometimes grateful. But the idea is to sponsor an evening that communicates to the participants that this is an *honest* global banquet. This is how eating looks in the world today, whether or not we see it.

Project 9: Tutoring for Life

One of the clearest predictors for poverty in the United States is level of education. People who graduate from college are not likely to experience poverty; a small percentage who graduate from high school will; and a future of poverty is virtually guaranteed for those who do not make it past junior high.

According to the U.S. Census Bureau, in 2004, at least 37 million Americans were living in poverty.[8] These are families that cannot afford to pay for the combined cost of rent, education, transportation, utilities, food and medical insurance. These are families that are, for the most part, working. Yet a prejudice against these individuals is common in our society: "If they would just get a job" or "If they would just take responsibility for themselves" are all too commonly heard about "these people."

It serves our purposes well to believe that people are poor for no other reason than the fact that they are lazy. But anyone who takes the time to encounter the reality of impoverished communities in the United States will discover wonderful, hard-working human beings who would give their right arm to overcome the poverty that defines their families' existence.

Our suggestion is to find ways to provide tutoring to those who are the most vulnerable. It's not the world's answer to overcoming poverty, but it is a specific, effective way to make a difference in a few people's lives.

If you are a student, the best way to start your tutoring career is to contact your university's education degree program department. Their staff members are typically in touch with local schools and neighborhoods where tutoring is needed (student teachers in their departments are often placed in those environments).

Another excellent way to find a tutoring slot is to visit your university's service-learning office. In addition to helping you connect with a program, service-learning departments usually provide transportation and can even place your tutoring service hours on your transcript. (That's always a plus when looking for a job or a graduate program that seeks only motivated, caring human beings.) You may also be able to connect with tutoring opportunities through the local school board, community service organizations or religious institutions.

Tutoring others will give you a better understanding of the material you are teaching and enrich your life. Tutoring is a very natural way to enter someone else's home or community. Solid, caring relationships are developed between tutors and students (and many times their parents as well), and these tutoring commitments often lead to long-term friendships.

Organizations

Beyond Borders
P.O. Box 2132
Norristown, PA 19404
Phone: 866-424-8403
E-mail: mail@beyondborders.net
Website: www.beyondborders.net

Bread for the World Institute
50 F Street, NW, Suite 500
Washington, DC 20001
Phone: 202-639-9400
Toll Free: 1-800-82-BREAD
Fax: 202-639-9401
E-mail: bread@bread.org
Website:
www.bread.org/about-us/institute/

**Harambee Family
Christian Center**
c/o Harambee Ministries
1609 Navarro Ave.
Pasadena, CA 91103
Phone: 626-798-7431
Fax: 626-798-1865
Website: www.harambee.org

Jubilee USA Network
222 East Capitol Street, NE
Washington, DC 20003
Phone: 202-783-3566
Fax: 202-546-4468
E-mail: coord@j2000usa.org
Website: www.jubileeusa.org

**New York City Coalition
Against Hunger**
16 Beaver St., 3rd Floor
New York, NY 10004
Phone: 212-825-0028
Fax: 212-825-0267
E-mail: info@nyccah.org
Website: www.nyccah.org

Target Earth International
P.O. Box 10777
Tempe, AZ 85284
Phone: 610-909-9740
Fax: 443-284-2399
E-mail: info@targetearth.org
Website: www.targetearth.org

World Concern
19303 Fremont Avenue North
Seattle, WA 98133
Phone: 206-546-7201
Toll Free: 1-800-755-5022
Fax: 206-546-7269
E-mail: info@worldconcern.org
Website: www.worldconcern.org

World Relief
7 East Baltimore Street
Baltimore, MD 21202
Phone: 443-451-1900
E-mail: worldrelief@wr.org
Website: www.wr.org

World Vision
United States Headquarters
P.O. Box 9716
Federal Way, WA 98063-9716
Phone: 888-511-6548
Fax: 253-815-1000
Website: www.worldvision.org

Evangelism

PROCLAIMING THE GOOD NEWS

Have you ever wondered why "man on the street" evangelism feels so unnatural? It is awkward to approach complete strangers and try to tell them in a few minutes' time that their lives are off track and need to be turned over to Jesus. It is also, for the most part, completely ineffective—most people don't like to be confronted on the street, and view such individuals who approach them as religious fanatics.

If you feel uncomfortable about employing this tactic, it is for a good reason: God never intended for evangelism to be a mini-sales presentation. Neither can we convince unbelieving people with debate and argument. Evangelism should feel as natural as breathing. In fact, sharing our faith is like *spiritual breathing*. All props aside, evangelism is that normal exchange we have with our surroundings. We take in, and we give out. And not surprisingly, it is this exchange that keeps us spiritually alive.

The Church in North America has largely failed in its evangelism efforts. This is a curious fact when you consider the billions of dollars we spend on outreach programs each year—building projects, radio, TV, literature, training seminars and crusades. Yet our society simply does not have the stamp of the Holy Spirit upon it. If all our programs led to spiritual life, we would not see such rampant deceit, violence, pornography, racism and other forms of injustice.

If the Church were more effective, we would see a society that reflects the fruit of the Holy Spirit: love, joy, peace, patience, kindness, goodness, faithfulness, gentleness and self-control (see Gal. 5:22-23). At the pragmatic level, we would see churches bursting with people who have traditionally found no home in the Church. However, most of the large congregations in our society are made up of people who have "moved over" from another fellowship.

It doesn't makes sense to harangue our church members into evangelistic programs any more than it does to beat the general population over the head and scream, "You must breathe, you idiots!" Our evangelism—our breathing, if you will—is living the life of a Spirit-filled Christian *in the presence of people outside the family of faith*. Too often we are trained to bombard people with our beliefs. We rush into their world with our doctrinal message and then escape to the safety of our churches once we have delivered the gospel message.

But evangelism is not a spiritual raid on the enemy—we are not meant to invade enemy territory or execute surgical strikes. Rather, we are called to live among the people who have not found the love of Jesus. Our life of love, tenderness and righteousness becomes the means by which the Holy Spirit woos them into the kingdom of God. No gimmicks here. We are talking about the demanding work of developing friendships with people who have not yet discovered that God is truly their best friend. This may sound rather simplistic, but remember that it was Jesus who said, "Let the little children come to me, and do not hinder them, for the kingdom of heaven belongs to such as these" (Matt. 19:14).

A song that some of us might have learned in Sunday School says, "This world is not my home, I'm just a-passin' through. My treasures are laid up, somewhere beyond the blue. The angels beckon me from heaven's open door, and I can't feel at home in this world anymore."[1] A great song, but it is only half true! Christians must live in the tension of *not* being at home while at the same time being at home.

This world is half our home. Christ has put us here for the purpose of planting our roots deep in the soil of contemporary society. By our persistent Spirit-filled living, we enlarge the influence of the Kingdom and demonstrate God's love to the world. Although we are told not to be *of* the world, we are called to live *in* the world. Maybe our traditional evangelistic programs serve as a trade-off: We like the security of the Church, but we feel we ought to do something about the people "out there." So we design ways to temporarily breathe.

We need to watch for places where the gospel might be absent and then pray for the courage and grace to live out our Christianity in that context. Our fellowship with Christians should model that same kind of lifestyle. Nothing could be more natural for a Christian.

Hopefully, as we become the presence of Jesus in society, we will be able to add those few words and warm hugs that help people make the final step into the arms of Jesus. *That* is evangelism at its best.

Project 1: Go Tell the News

Estimates indicate that as many as 250,000 local church members have taken part in various short, international and cross-cultural trips.[2] There is good reason for this, of course: In our day of rapid transportation and modern technology, it makes sense to explore new cultures. God has gifted us with curious minds and has put within us a love for the world.

A huge benefit of going overseas and serving people in some capacity is its life-changing value to the people who participate. Many pastors and church leaders are deeply committed to these cross-cultural excursions for their congregations for no other reason than they light a fire inside their church members. A pastor-friend of ours says it is *the* key to his discipleship program and that it would be the church's last budget item to go.

Going on short-term evangelism trips can provide excellent opportunities for people to sharpen their commitment, gain courage and experience God's faithfulness in their lives. Although we must be careful not to fall into the trap of thinking that we can only do evangelism in a foreign land, these kinds of international trips can be powerful. We regularly hear stories about people who come back from these trips with a new energy. They return revitalized and excited, perhaps because their hearts have been given a jump-start and they now recognize the true nature of their faith.

Sound like an awakening that you could use? Here are a few organizations that you could partner with to take evangelism on the road:

- **Youth With A Mission (YWAM).** YWAM leads people on regular outreach trips ranging in length from one week to two years. YWAM has locations all over the world and they train students and people of all ages in the areas of discipleship, evangelism and other forms of ministry. Check them out at www.ywam.org.

- **Youth for Christ:** Youth for Christ leads various short-term trips including medical mission trips, mission trips to do construction, and evangelistic mission trips. Youth for Christ provides opportunities to do international missions work in Africa, South America, Asia, the Pacific and Europe as well as domestic missions work here in the United States. Visit their website at www.yfc.net.

- **Vacation With a Purpose.** The Vacation With a Purpose program was originally established to provide church members with opportunities to go on meaningful vacations in which they helped those in need. The idea was a great success, and now many churches around the country have adopted the program. One such program can be found at the Highland Park Methodist Church website at www.hppc.org.

- **Bridge Builders.** Bridge Builders is a one-stop resource for short-term mission needs. The organization will custom-make a trip specifically for members of a church and offer a full range of services from booking tickets to designing the program and from teaching the devotionals to coordinating the construction effort. The staff at Bridge Builders listens carefully to what people want and then creates the package around that request. Visit the organization's website at www.bridgebuilders.org.

- **Discover the World.** Discover the World is an organization that sends teams into churches to train members on how to run their own programs. Although Discover the World does not broker specific experiences, it will train teams and provide Bible study materials for them to take abroad. You can find out more at www.discover theworld.org.

- **NieuCommunities.** NieuCommunities is a division of Church Resource Ministries (CRM), an organization that ministers in major metropolitan regions of the United States and in 21 countries around the world. Nieu-Communities leads people on 42-week-long outreach trips or on shorter 1- to 2-week "road trips" to places such as Vancouver, Canada; Pretoria, South Africa; and Glasgow, Scotland. To contact NieuCommunities, go to www.nieu communities.org.

Jesus sent His disciples on short-term missions trips (see Luke 10). So if it worked for the Master, it can work for us too!

Project 2: Leave the Church

This idea may sounds strange, but it's a serious evangelistic notion. We all need to consciously leave the security of fellow believers and put ourselves in an environment where Christ intends the Church to live. Here are several ways to help you make the first step to get outside of the church walls:

- **Volunteer in Your Community.** Find out if your area has an inner-city ministry or organization that helps or evangelizes people in the city. Arrange to volunteer with this organization for a weekend, or at least 2 or 3 days in a row. Or if you find a group that you like, spend a summer volunteering once or twice a week.

- **Go Outside Your Comfort Zone.** Think about several groups whose members are typically unlike your regular circle of friends. Perhaps they have different political views or are part of a vocation that is unfamiliar to you.

Find out where they gather and attend their events. Learn about their beliefs and activities, and listen to their needs and aspirations. Pray for sensitivity to their way of viewing life. Volunteer to help them with projects that do not directly conflict with your own values. It will be surprising how much you'll learn in a short amount of time.

- **Join a Club.** If you enjoy sports, join a local club. Surround yourself with people you don't know and pray for opportunities to meet new people. Pray for each person you meet, whether he or she becomes a friend or just a regular gym partner. If sports are not your thing, join a local society or service organization that fits your interests, such Toastmasters, PTA, Lions Club, Big Brothers or Big Sisters. Pray for genuine new acquaintances and look for opportunities to make friends and serve people you do not know.

- **Open Up.** Open your home to your neighbors. In the summer, invite them over for a barbecue. Host a party for them in your home on special national occasions such as the Fourth of July, Thanksgiving, Mother's Day, or another holiday. As Christians, we need to be showing this kind of genuine hospitality.

In all of these endeavors, it is important to be genuine as you make friends. Remember, it is not necessary to jump into an unnatural evangelistic relationship. In time, God will allow your life to become sweet aroma and water for a thirsty heart. Let that be a natural process guided by the work of the Holy Spirit. With His guidance, it will be clear when and how to add life-giving words to your lifestyle.

One other thought: It is tempting to think that people who have different Christian beliefs do not know Jesus, but in fact this could be nothing more than a form of spiritual prejudice. We encourage you to surround yourself with people whose views appear to be in conflict with your own. There are at least two good reasons for this: (1) you may be surprised to see how much they love Jesus, and (2) you will gain a more honest view of the "other side."

Project 3: Practice Hospitality

Imagine hardened leaders of a labor union meeting for prayer and Bible study in the basement of a church. This kind of thing actually happens!

A friend of ours is a leader in a church located across the street from a business that was recently the target of a strike. Every day, the organized workers walked up and down the sidewalk with placards bearing messages about unfair labor contracts. Some mean tactics were being used against those employees who crossed the picket lines, and church and civil leaders (our friend included) condemned the behavior of the strike leaders.

The strike lasted into the winter. On one bitterly cold morning, the Lord prompted our friend to offer the church building as a place of warmth for the strikers. Did he respond, *You've got to be kidding Lord?!* Nope. He set up a coffee table in the church basement and went over to the very people he had condemned, inviting them to use the church—coffee and all—as needed to take shelter from the cold.

The invitation was enthusiastically received, and soon the church became a regular place of relief and relaxation. Church members began to mix with the strikers, and before long, the members' prejudices began to slip away as real men and women replaced the caricatures they had created in their minds of the hardened labor leaders.

The strike lasted that entire winter, and all of the unstructured downtime allowed for hearty arguments about life and faith. Halfway into the winter, several strikers joined our friend for a special Bible study each morning. He was able to pray with these people who were experiencing the economic crunch of the strike. Church members visited family members who were sick, and some of the families even started coming to the church.

What went on in this situation? The church was willing to follow Jesus' words, "Love your enemies, do good to them, and lend to them without expecting to get anything back" (Luke 6:35). Most of us would naturally provide shelter for our friends, but Jesus wants us to do the same for those whom we do not call friends. This sort of hospitality is at the heart of what it means to be a Christian and lays the groundwork for leading others to Christ. Our friend was responding to the Lord's nudges. The genuine, loving nature of his deeds spoke of the substance of the gospel clearly and paved the way for evangelism.

There are many ways you can provide hospitality to the people with whom you come into contact each day. Is there a classmate at school who seems lonely or depressed? Take the initiative to get to know that person over a cup of coffee. Is there a person in your church who could use your help with a project? Volunteer your time and expertise. As we mentioned in chapter 1, serving soup kitchens and other volunteer projects for the homeless is an excellent way to show hospitality. In one church, members organized a dinner each week and brought the food to the local park where the homeless gather. Such acts of hospitality not only provide an excellent witness for the love of Christ but also serve to change some people's stereotypes regarding these individuals in our society.

These simple acts of love cut across the hurried and often harsh pace of life. Showing love to fellow human beings is all too scarce in our world today. And who better than the family of God to communicate this message?

Project 4: Focus on Unreached Peoples

If there is such a thing as the final frontier of missions, it is those areas outside the shadow of the Church. Today, 2.1 billion people in the world are considered unreached—people who have never heard the gospel and have no idea what or who Jesus is.[3]

Missionary work to the unreached peoples of the world is perhaps the closest we can get to the older model of missions. This work often requires building relationships with people in closed societies who are suspicious of foreigners, who do not employ modern technology, and who live in a tightly knit web of relationships in which conversion to Christ means the rejection of their family. This is a notion very unfamiliar to our society.

Preparing yourself to become involved in missions to unreached peoples is no small task. The commitment requires immense preparation, study and training. Mission assignments are typically long-term, which cuts against our cultural norm that emphasizes mobility and having shallow roots. Yet ministering to unreached people groups provides many exciting and rich opportunities.

Several organizations that can help you realize some of the benefits of long-term missions work and provide you with additional resources include:

- **Zwemer Institute.** The Zwemer Institute is the nation's leading center for orienting Christians to work with Muslims. Their staff can give you detailed information about ministering to Muslims at your church or simply provide you with information to share with your church leaders. Their seminars are especially good at teaching people to appreciate the immense contributions that Arabs have made to Western society. For more information, visit the Zwemer Center for Muslim Studies' website at www.ciu.edu/muslimstudies.

- **Frontiers.** Frontiers is another ministry to unreached peoples, specifically Muslims. The ministry offers opportunities for short-term missions trips, internships, apprenticeships, long-term trips and even church-based ministry. Check out their website at www.frontiers.org.

- **U.S. Center for World Mission.** The U.S. Center for World Mission has a college-level course called "Perspectives on the World Christian Movement" that is taught annually in 150 different locations around the world. Since its inception, more than 60,000 people have taken the class. The course consists of 20 lectures spread over 10 weeks, including reading assignments and tests (classes typically meet for 10 Monday nights in a row, with each evening lasting 3 1/2 hours). College credit is available for those who take this seminar. Often, churches will cosponsor the course, so perhaps you can find a church in your area offering it. You can check out the class and find other information on missions at the U.S. Center for World Mission's website at www.perspectives.org.

Project 5: Give to Missions

There is no doubt that sending out missionaries to other nations is expensive. Some people argue that it is poor stewardship to support missionaries when nationals can do the same job for much less money. If we looked only at the economic grid, this would be true. For example, the salary package of one U.S. missionary family in India could support 30 missionary families in India doing the identical work. But we cannot always look at economics.

Because each person in the Body of Christ brings unique gifts to God's work in the world, we should not underestimate the value that missionaries from our country can bring to other unreached peoples. Furthermore, a global outlook on the work of missions forces people to look outside of themselves to see the situations of other people around the world. When missionaries are sent into those nations, they serve to strengthen the global unity of the Body of Christ and further the work of God on this earth. For these reasons, we must continue to support Western missionaries, even if the bill seems extreme.

Having said that, it is true that there are many advantages to supporting the efforts of missionaries seeking to spread the gospel in their native countries. Native missionaries have few or no cultural barriers to hinder their work. They typically speak the language of the people to whom they are witnessing or have other resources that they can use to communicate the message of Christ. They are often more accepted than outsiders to the country and have a greater understanding of the challenges in that particular environment.

Yet there is very little direct support to nationals who are doing the work of missions. In fact, funds sent to these individuals for the purpose of increasing local evangelism efforts in their countries are often handled by agencies that siphon off questionable chunks for overhead. Instead of being specifically used to promote the gospel by local missionaries, the money is used to fund other projects deemed important by the organization.

One group we believe is doing a unique work that could benefit from the gracious giving of the North American Church is Gospel for Asia. This ministry, which is operated by an Indian man, has more than 3,000 full-time missionaries. The organization's primary goal is to plant churches among the unreached and fund native missionaries to work in their own countries. *One hundred percent* of the donations received by Gospel for Asia go directly into the field—none of it is siphoned off for administrative expenses or used for other purposes. When you support Gospel for Asia, you can be assured that any money donated will be used with the utmost integrity and will go far in touching people's lives. You can visit the organization's website at www.gfa.org.

Whether you support Gospel for Asia or another organization, we recommend that you look for organizations that are empowering and supporting native missionaries whenever possible.

Organizations

Big Brothers and Big Sisters
230 North 13th Street
Philadelphia, PA 19107
Phone: 215-567-7000
Fax: (215) 567-0394
Website: www.bbbs.org

Bridge Builders
P.O. Box 76299
St. Petersburg, FL 33734
Phone: 727-551-9060
Fax: 727-551-9073
Website: www.bridgebuilders.org

Discover the World
3255 E. Orange Grove Blvd.
Pasadena, CA 91107
Phone: 626-577-9502
Fax: 626-796-4447
Website: www.discovertheworld.org

Frontiers
P.O. Box 31690
Mesa, AZ 85275-1690
Phone: 480-834-1500
Toll-Free: 800-462-8436
E-mail: info@frontiers.org
Website: www.frontiers.org

Gospel for Asia
1932 Walnut Plaza
Carrollton, TX 75006
Phone: 972-300-7777
Toll-Free: 800-946-2742
Website: www.gfa.org

**National Parent Teacher
Association (PTA)**
Attn: Customer Service Department
541 North Fairbanks Court, Suite 1300
Chicago, IL 60611
Phone: 312-670-6782

Toll-Free: 800-307-4PTA
Fax: 312-670-6783
Website: www.pta.org

NieuCommunities
c/o Church Resource Ministries
1240 N. Lakeview Avenue, Suite 120
Anaheim, CA 92807
Phone: 800-777-6658
E-mail: charlie.johnson@crmleaders.org
Website: www.nieucommunities.org

Lions Club International
Extension and Membership Division
300 West 22nd Street
Oak Brook, IL
Phone: 630-571-5466
Website: www.lionsclubs.org

Toastmasters International
P.O. Box 9052
Mission Viejo, CA 92690
Phone: 949-858-8255 or 949-835-1300
Fax: 949-858-1207
Website: www.toastmasters.org

Youth for Christ
P.O. Box 4478
Englewood, CO 80155
Phone: 303-843-9000
Fax: 303-843-9002
E-mail: info@yfc.com
Website: www.yfc.net

Youth With A Mission (YWAM)
YWAM Campaigns
708 Main Street
Grandview, MO 64030
Phone: 816-795-1500
Fax: 816-795-6568
Website: www.ywam.org

The Environment

TENDING GOD'S CREATION

Sit back for a moment and reflect on all the details and complexities that went into the process of the creation of the world. God specifically penciled out the shape of each of the millions of flowers on Earth, blended the watercolors and matched the leaves to the petals. He decided which varieties should grow in the various climates, how they should group themselves on the edge of a hill in early spring, and how they should lay a carpet across a meadow. He added trees and shrubs and brushed in hundreds of varieties of grasses. He strategically placed waterfalls, rivers and underground springs to bubble over the rocks and provide sustenance to the delicate plants.

And that is just the beginning. Consider all the diverse flocks of birds, ducks and geese that are in this world. Picture the design and placement of jaguars, foxes, raccoons, badgers, elephants and deer. Sink into the deep oceans and imagine the millions of colorful fishes and sea creatures that swim in an underground world of delight that is much like a private aquarium for the Creator.

Design a sunset. Create a sunrise. Push the ocean's floor up through billions of tons of water and make an island from molten rock. Dot the sky with stars overhead. Place the planets with their mystical rings and moons in orbit. All of Creation is the personal handiwork of the same God who was viciously strung up on a piece of wood.

Yet it is curious how many Christians do not seem to care about being good stewards of God's creation. "This is my Father's world," says the hymn, and so it is.[1] Scripture proclaims, "The earth is the LORD's, and the fullness thereof" (Ps. 24:1, *KJV*). People who love Jesus should no more destroy the environment than rip to shreds the carefully painted canvas of a best friend. It is nothing but pure blasphemy to disrespect the creative work of God.

The Church has been silent for far too long on this issue. We have allowed those outside the faith to define our obligation to care for the garden. We have, in fact, withdrawn from our duty to tend it. Worse, we have often labeled people who *do* care for the earth as "liberal," or something worse.

When we care for the environment, we show our deep respect for the Creator in much the same way we would admire the work of a great artist in a museum. When we fail to care for our planet, the world sees our treatment of Creation and unconsciously picks up the message regarding our disrespect. When we care about God's handiwork, we demonstrate our love for God. And that speaks volumes to the world.

What is more, caring for Creation is a way of caring for ourselves. Nature has a way of ministering back to us. It provides color, shapes, scents, shade and sustenance. And by tending Creation, we also show consideration for our children's future. We demonstrate that we love them enough to provide a clean and beautiful garden that paints a stunning picture of the Artist.

There is nothing suspicious about loving the environment, but there is something awfully suspicious and wrong about trampling it. Doesn't it make sense that those who personally love the Creator would be the ones to take a personal interest in His handiwork?

Next time you pass a rose, stop and smell it. After all, it's naturally Christian to do so.

Project 1: Green Your City

Christians sometimes find it difficult to find common ground with people outside their faith. One way to come together with those who might not be Christians is to simply care for the earth by "greening" your city or community. There is no catch to this project—no literature or speeches that try to convince people to join the faith—but the result is a wonderful place of beauty for whoever wants to enjoy it.

There are several ways to green your city. Some ideas are listed below, starting with the simplest to the more complex. Pick the level that suits your situation. You may want to gather a group of friends, recruit members from your church, or join with other church groups in your region to take on the more ambitious projects. Whatever level you choose, remember to first approach the officials at your local city hall to ask them what you can do. Approach them with a clear offer: "We want to help keep the city beautiful—nothing more. We are offering to do the planning, the work. What can we do?"

- **Adopt a Block.** Landscape the sidewalks or medians of a specific section of town—perhaps even a couple of city blocks. Some communities already have adopt-a-block programs. If there is one in your area, maybe your friends or your small group or college group can join one. If there is not, maybe you can be the first to adopt a block in your city.

- **Stage a Cleanup.** Offer to stage a trash cleanup event with your group in an area of your city that desperately needs to be picked clean of trash and rubbish. Sometimes a city will even supply the trash bins if you provide the volunteers to haul trash. Gather your group, bring gloves and good attitudes, and clean up!

- **Plant a Tree.** Plant trees on city- or county-owned property that is unlikely to be developed. Make it an annual event rather than a one-time event. You will need to coordinate with city planners to find out the areas available and the types of trees and shrubs they would like to have planted.

- **Do Some Landscaping.** Landscape a city monument or historical building. City budgets are shrinking all the time, so your local officials will probably be happy to have someone lend a hand. This allows for a lot of creative expression for any of your friends who might be gardeners or green thumbs.

- **Create a Minipark.** This is not a large recreational facility, of course, but a walk-and-sit kind of place where you bring your picnic basket for a slow lunch. If the land is designed well, you could include a small pond with ducks and fish.

If you take on one of the larger projects, you may want to look for professionals in your church or school who are knowledgeable in horticulture, landscaping, architecture or other kinds of planning. Cities have to watch out for liability and labor concerns, so don't get frustrated if you can't immediately find a project to tackle. Start small with a project, such as a trash cleanup, that you can complete on your own and without permission from your city. You can still make your city beautiful in the process!

Project 2: Green Your Church or School

One of the benefits of the environmental movement is that it has taught ordinary folks—not just the experts—that we are all able to make a difference.

One way that you can make a difference in your own community is to volunteer to make sure your church or school's habits are friendly to the environment. By doing so, you will be instituting patterns that can become a daily reminder that you worship the Lord of Creation—and therefore are taking good care of His "garden." Some of the ways that you can help green your church or school include:

- **Reduce Paperwork.** Whenever possible, use PowerPoint slides instead of handouts. Project announcements or any materials you are using for a presentation on a screen instead of printing them on a sheet of paper.

- **Avoid Waste.** Be careful to avoid waste at any church or school functions you coordinate. When possible, use plates, cups and silverware that can be washed. And stamp out Styrofoam altogether—it is almost impossible to recycle.

- **Create a System.** Create a simple recycling system, if there isn't one in place, to collect all newspapers, magazines, used office paper and junk mail. These can be recycled. Ask the leadership of your school or church if you can post a few signs to make the case for recycling.

If you are a student, one idea for getting your university involved in recycling efforts is to ask the leadership of your institution to participate in an event called RecycleMania. RecycleMania is a 10-week competition in which schools compete to see which university can collect the largest amount of recyclables and generate the least amount of trash. Trophies and prizes are awarded, but the main goal of the event is to increase student awareness of the amount of waste generated on our nation's campuses.

In 2006, approximately 100 schools participated in the event. For more information and resources on recycling, visit the RecycleMania website at www.recyclemaniacs.com.

Project 3: Celebrate Earth Day

For more than 30 years, Earth Day (April 22) has provided a way for people to focus national attention on issues that concern our environment. Back in the early days, the focus of this day was on a global vision of all human beings living in harmony with the earth. Space travel had recently brought us pictures of our world, and for the first time people saw what a truly small and finite piece of galactic furniture our planet really was. *Surely*, people thought, *we could all figure out how to make this planet habitable for all its members and for all generations.*

Twenty years ago, care of the environment was not as politicized as it is today. In the early 1970s, Republican president Richard Nixon introduced the Clean Air Act and the Clean Water Act and pushed for the protection of species, habitat and national physical wonders. Back then, you didn't have to be politically liberal to value the earth, and you didn't have to choose business over the environment to be politically conservative. Later, another Republican president even dispatched his economic team to advise countries on how to develop their coastal zones away from the water's edge, specifically to avoid the potential impact of global warming and rising sea levels.

Today, the nation is traveling through a particularly mean-spirited period in which the dollar is truly lord of all life. There's very little blush in the faces of corporate leaders and government officials who encourage the wanton destruction of the earth if it can provide short-term profits in their coffers. Indeed, in 2006, ExxonMobil distinguished itself by having the greatest net profit of any company in the history of the world (more than $35 billion in one year).[2] The company spent millions of dollars in prior years funding groups and foundations with the goal of debunking research on how the planet was being adversely and dangerously affected by carbon emissions. In an article in the *Wall Street Journal*, Jeffery Ball wrote:

> Openly and unapologetically, the world's No. 1 oil company disputes the notion that fossil fuels are the main cause of global warming. Along with the Bush administration, Exxon opposes the Kyoto accord and the very idea of capping global-warming emissions. . . . Exxon also contributes money to think tanks and other groups that agree with its stance.[3]

The bottom line for these guys (which is what most of them are) seems to be more money at whatever cost to the earth.

Earth Day is a good annual plumb line for a nation so caught up in destructive consumerism. It's a moment to be reminded that we are more than the mean-spirited monster chomping its way through everyone else's garden in the global village. Earth Day is a great time to provide general public education on the environment, launch specific campaigns on contemporary needs, and put our elected officials on notice that we are not willing to live as thoughtlessly as some would suggest fits the American ideal.

To really get into the spirit of Earth Day, consider volunteering at an Earth Day event in your city or region. Volunteer to do a local trash cleanup, start a recycling program and use more recycled goods, plant trees, learn how to keep your house plants growing with less water, dispose of toxins properly, and discover ways to minimize the amount of time you drive your car. You can do these things each day of the year, or you pick one at a time and implement it into your daily routine.

One of the easiest Earth Day projects that you can do right now is to reduce the amount of energy you use in your home. Begin by replacing the light bulbs in your house or apartment with Compact Fluorescent Light Bulbs (CFLs), which last longer and use less energy. In fact, the Earth Day Network estimates that if every household in the United States replaced just one light bulb with a CFL, it would eliminate the equivalent of the emissions caused by one million cars.[4]

The single greatest energy eater in your home is probably your refrigerator, so reduce the energy used in this giant appliance by lowering the thermostat one or two degrees. Have your refrigerator's condenser coil cleaned and keep it out of the sun and away from heater vents. Make sure the door is always closed and tightly sealed at all times. And if you have two refrigerators, get rid of one.

Other ways to save energy in your home include turning down your hot-water heater a few degrees, only running a load of dishes if your dishwasher is full (or doing them by hand), and washing your clothes in warm instead of hot water (this single act can cut your energy use by 50 percent). Also, if you can stand it, try to reduce the amount of time throughout the year that you use heating and cooling systems.

One of the best ways to get involved—especially if there isn't a designated Earth Day event in your area—is to volunteer to organize an Earth Day event for your city. There is no shortage of organizations for good resources on Earth Day celebrations, including helpful websites such as www.earthday.gov, www.earth day.net and www.earthdaybags.org.

One group that we'd recommend in particular is the Environmental Defense Fund, which is an excellent resource on global climate change, species protection and more. Its origins, just a decade prior to Earth Day, centered around a campaign to eliminate DDT—a spray freely used to kill mosquitoes that proved to be a deadly toxin in the food chain. You can contact the Environmental Defense Fund at www.environmentaldefense.org.

Project 4: Noah's Ark

Most ancient traditions have stories about protecting animals and plants. Whether the saving act is for the species themselves or because of some use they bring to humans, the idea of ridding the world of everything but humans and a few crops on which they depend has never been a praiseworthy vision.

Yet in some circles of contemporary Western society, there are leaders (both economic and religious) who seem very comfortable with the idea of allowing progress to drive great numbers of species into extinction. The attitudes of these leaders represent the worst kind of arrogance in our society. When God placed humankind as the keeper of His creation, He intended for us to take dominion over it (see Gen. 1:28) and to take care of it (see Gen. 2:15)—not make ourselves lord over it. We have made ourselves the focal point to such a degree that we may as well declare that the earth revolves around us.

Our modern society has pursued an unprecedented course of ridding the earth of its marvelous diversity. A conservative estimate by the World Conservation Union suggests that we are destroying more than 16,000 species as a result of our lifestyles encroaching on their habitats.[5] Surely it was never in our minds and hearts that the "benefits" of contemporary life included the destruction of so much beauty. Yet at the same time, it is not clear what kind of spiritual poverty leaves us unmoved by such loss of beauty.

Beyond the beauty, there are, of course, human benefits to keeping species alive. The glamorous examples are species that have value to us medicinally. In remote parts of the world, scientists have found agents from plants and trees that counter certain cancers and heart and kidney disorders. We also know that many species are members of a complex, integrated system of ecology that keeps the earth alive, vibrant and viable.

When we rob the earth of a species, we eliminate a key component of its health. We would consider a person who thoughtlessly cut out his liver or spleen to be crazy, yet we systematically cut out parts of the body of this earth upon which our very future depends. As we pour toxins into rivers and oceans, cut down immense tracts of the rainforest, pave over valleys and hills and suck aquifers dry, we are destroying the habitats of our life partners. Surely, if beauty were not enough of a reason to preserve the diversity of this earth, the future of our grandkids should be.

There are many ways to get involved to help protect animals and plants. A primary way is to write letters to your senators and congressmen about protecting America's public lands and wildlife preserves, confronting global warming, and preserving the Endangered Species Act. Another way to help is to volunteer with a local wildlife society, which will also help you engage in your local community and raise your general awareness level.

Three organizations that provide helpful information on endangered species include the World Wildlife Fund, the National Wildlife Federation, and the World Conservation

Union. The World Wildlife Fund attempts to raise awareness of the plight of a few key species such as the Giant Panda, Bengal Tiger and African Elephant. The organization's notion is that the loss of those large species will alert us to much greater losses in those habitats of lesser-known species. It's a great way to make the case for entire ecosystem health. More information regarding the World Wildlife Fund can be found at www.worldwildlife.org.

The second organization, the National Wildlife Federation, is another group that has a strong history of protecting species. The organization takes on specific campaigns and puts together action packets and resource guides. On their website, you can find links to your regional lawmakers, sample letters to help get you started writing to your senators and congressmen, and detailed information and resources for your campaign. You can reach the National Wildlife Federation through the group's website at www.nwf.org.

The third organization, the World Conservation Union (also known as the International Union of Nature and Natural Resources), is the world's largest conservation network. The organization attempts to influence societies around the world to conserve the integrity and diversity of nature by supporting and developing conservation science, implementing this research in projects around the world, and working with governments to create policies that protect the environment. Each year, the World Conservation Union publishes the "Red List," which classifies species according to their extinction risk. Photographs of endangered species and other helpful resources are available at the organization's website at www.iucn.org.

Project 5: Cut the Trash

America constitutes about 5 percent of the world's population, yet we consume approximately 30 percent of the world's resources.

We also produce approximately 19 percent of the world's trash.[6]

In past years, the dominant economic theory in America was that we needed to increase consumption in order to drive the economic engine of the world, which in turn was supposed to create a higher standard of living for everyone. That way of thinking is becoming less credible as the world begins to groan from the weight of overconsumption. Our rainforests are being cut down at unprecedented rates, rivers and oceans are being treated as gigantic garbage dumps for our commercial waste, the air is choking from all the pollution we belch into the sky from our factories and cars, and species are dying off at a high rate as we destroy their habitats.

Part of the myth that drives overconsumption is that all of this extra stuff will somehow make our lives better and our spirits happier. This myth is too costly to the earth and to our souls.

One important way to be kind to the earth is to simply *use less of it*. Some of the ways to begin to make a difference in the world today include:

- **Refuse**. Just say no. Don't buy something just because you can or because you want it. Every time you buy something, you are using up a piece of the earth and causing pollution.

- **Reduce**. If you cannot say no, perhaps you can reduce your rate of consumption. For example, how about using half of a tank of gas this week rather than three-quarters of a tank of gas? How about reading a newspaper at a library instead of purchasing your own private copy?

- **Reuse**. Sometimes waste is just so meaningless. When you throw out a bottle after drinking its contents, it's no different from throwing out a mug at the restaurant after drinking the coffee from it! It wasn't so long ago that Americans found a second use for almost everything—string, cardboard, the Sunday paper, plastic lids, and so on. So why not give something a second and a third life?

- **Recycle.** This is the bottom of the hierarchy—the last stop. It's better to just say no for starters, but if you can't (or if you have already reduced and reused), you can often recycle something instead of just throwing it in the trash bin. Recycling gives someone else the chance to figure out how to reuse that item which is no longer useful to you.

Two nonprofit groups that have many good ideas and resources related to cutting down the waste in our lives and living more sensitively and meaningfully are the New American Dream and Adbusters. The first group, the New American Dream, attempts to redefine what it means to live out the grand American dream in ways that are not hurtful to the environment. For more information, visit the group's website at www. newdream.org.

The second group, Adbusters, is an innovative company that looks at how the economic machine attempts to get Americans to consume more. The company gets behind the psychology of ad campaigns and tries to expose the values that drive high levels of consumption. They even remake advertisements as parodies! For ideas and insights from the company's efforts, visit their website at www.adbusters.org.

Project 6: Take a Bike

One of the best ways to be kind to the environment is to reduce carbon emissions. The car is a chief culprit in creating air pollution;

yet the bind is, as some have noted, that America has historically had a love affair with the motorcar.

It's not as if car pollution is a problem we have just discovered. Fifteen years ago, the city of Los Angeles noted high rates of lung particulate disorder among children—a consequence of stifling air pollution. Schools literally had to establish a color-flag system to instruct their students when it was "safe" to be outdoors. A green flag indicated that the air-quality index was good; yellow indicated that it was moderate; orange meant the air was unhealthy for sensitive people; and a red flag signaled that the air was unhealthy for everyone.[7]

With all of our assertions around the benefits of modern technology, somewhere in the discussion we need to be clear about the true costs of our romantic vision of modernization. We label cigarette packets about the dangers of inhaling tobacco. But some cities have to put labels on the atmosphere!

One way that you can help to reduce carbon emissions and improve the quality of the air is to join with millions of Americans who are discovering a new love affair—the bike. Cycling to work, to school or to a friend's house can be a practical and, at the same time, healthy way of commuting around town. Of course, it's not always convenient to bike everywhere (although some hardy folks would beg to differ). Some cities are not set up to accommodate cyclists, and some weather patterns don't make for safe riding, either. That aside, there is a growing movement in America for people to leave the car in the garage.

One innovative group that is pushing for more cycling is Yellow Bikes (a takeoff of Yellow Cabs), headquartered in St. Paul, Minnesota. The group's initial idea was to create a large pool of reconditioned bikes for free public use in cities across America. People could simply pick up a bike at a predetermined location and drop it off when they were done. Because of the group's efforts, many bikes that would have ended up in landfills have gained a second lease on life, and a lot of cars have been given the day off on a regular basis. Yellow Bikes has spread to many cities across the country. The idea has taken a slightly different shape in each city, but the goal is always the same: to reduce car pollution. In some cities, you can rent a bike for a day, lease it for a week, or even plan a group event at which several people go out biking together.

If you don't want to join Yellow Bikes (or there is not one located in your area), you can still help the environment by simply giving your car a break now and then. Find a way to use your car less and find a way to cycle more. (Increased gas prices are reason enough for most of us right now, but clean air is not a bad reason either!) College campuses tend to be very friendly toward bicycle use for individuals, and with so many people coming together in one spot each day, a collective use of bikes would be easy enough to establish.

Contact Yellow Bikes for ideas on how to make the most of cycling. The organization's official headquarters is now in St. Paul, Minnesota (and you know how much snow and ice blankets that city in the winter). The web address is www.yellowbikes.org.

Project 7: Be Kind to Animals

According to the United States Department of Agriculture's Animal Welfare Enforcement, in 2001 more than one million animals (including dogs, cats, guinea pigs, primates, hamsters and rabbits) were used for experiments in the United States.[8] The animals were used to test shampoos, soaps, repellants, food products and a number of other items.

The majority of people in the world do not struggle with the idea of killing animals for food, but few would agree that animals should be subject to cruel, painful treatment simply to increase a person's options in life. Baby seal cubs are clubbed to death by the hundreds of thousands each year in fishing communities. Live cats are thrown in boiling water by the thousands to harvest their pelts for fur coats. Millions of animals are stuffed into feedlots for burgers, and hundreds of millions of chickens go through their entire lifespan without being able to walk. Labs pour toxins and soaps into the eyes of rabbits to see what adverse affects the product could inflict on humans. And thousands of animals are injected annually with increasing dosages of poisons until the animal dies—apparently to test the threshold of tolerance for substances that industry plans to use in public.

Sound like the Garden of Eden?

There's a certain edge to human arrogance that views animals as a simple resource to be exploited at all costs. Some humans have developed a kind of dominion ideology in which they believe that they have the ethical right to do with animals as they please. No compassion or moral thought enters their minds as they treat animals with total disregard.

We have three specific suggestions for being kind to animals. The first is about finding ways to change your personal lifestyle so that you can go through life's normal consuming demands without inflicting pain on animals. One organization that is devoted to kindness to animals is People for the Ethical Treatment of Animals (PETA). The organization posts both the good and the ugly on its website, where you can find the latest campaigns against companies that violate animals, learn which food and clothing products are created without animal testing, and discover other resources for further education. Make a commitment with what you learn from the PETA website to buy only certain kinds of products. In some cases, you may have to pay a little more. In most cases, you'll just have to change some of your patterns or tastes.

Next, conduct an education campaign on your campus. Set up a creative booth at the student mall or other public place where you can show videos (PETA has plenty), display posters, or hand out relevant literature. You'd be surprised how many students are not aware of the price that animals pay to maintain people's lifestyle in our society. Be creative. One student group brought pets on campus and put them in cages with their bodies marked up for experimentation. Another group built a mock pain threshold panel and hooked up stuffed pets to it, as if they were testing the animal's response to increased toxin shots. The same group of students smashed in the heads of stuffed animals with hammers. Next to the table they had a sign that read, "Test center for cranial strength."

The final suggestion is to sign people up for current animal cruelty campaigns. PETA and related sites track court cases and legislation linked to animal treatment. You can host booths at your campus to get petitions signed, letters generated and votes cast. For all of these suggestions and more, go to People for the Ethical Treatment of Animals at www.peta.org.

Project 8: Drop Down the Food Chain

There was a time in human history when the scale of human population to the globe was fairly minimal. No one considered the idea that the earth would one day groan under the impact of our lives. But we don't live in that kind of world anymore. To support our local wants, we have to go to other people's backyards and take what is not ours.

For example, entire swaths of the rainforest are being destroyed in South America to support cattle production for hamburger sales in the United States. Do we really want to pay that kind of ethical price for a burger? And, of course, destroying those forests has negative impacts on the rest of the world, which depends upon the Amazon for carbon fixing and global rain patterns.

The culture of America is one of limitless possibilities. We live with the notion that there is always a solution around the corner and another technical fix that can get us out of a prior fix. But that's not a reasonable position to hold when our fix includes wrecking other people's land, polluting their rivers, and destroying their natural wonders. Our romance with technology is not honest. This past century has introduced more types of toxic chemicals into our blood vessels than all previous centuries in history put together. Where do we get our idea that this is progress?

One sensible way of being easier on the earth is by *eating lower on the food chain*. Most kids are taught the "food pyramid" in school. Although there is some debate as to what foods are the healthiest for our bodies, the pyramid is a helpful tool in understanding what categories of food are necessary for nutrition. In the same way, the food chain is a helpful tool for helping measure the environmental costs associated with the production of food. When a person consumes food that is lower on the food chain, the less impact his or her nutritional intake has upon the environment. One way to ensure a healthy planet for the future is to find that intersection of eating in which we are taking in all the nutrients we need while at the same time securing that food from a source that has the least drain on the earth.

Central to the principle of eating lower on the food chain is the idea of lessening each person's net impact upon the earth. Here's one way to think of it: What is the most efficient means of getting meat protein? Well, ounce for ounce of net protein, it takes 13 times as much grain to feed a cow as it does a chicken. When you add to that the other costs of feeding cows versus chickens (barns, fences, fields, fuel, equipment, staffing), the cost of cow protein becomes much higher. So, if we are able to get the same nutritional value into our bodies from a bite of chicken as we can from a bite of beef, why not use that means and preserve the earth?

The key to eating low on the food chain is to gain proteins from "low cost" sources. In fact, you don't even have to eat meat for protein—you can get all the protein you need from a combination of grains and legumes. If you do eat meat, you can make a habit of eating chicken or fish more than beef. (Your doctor will tell you that all of your body's protein needs for one day can be satisfied with one bite of chicken—it's not as though we have to eat a side of beef to stay healthy!) The idea here is not to be legalistic about food but to be sensible and creative. What could be so wrong about trying to be careful with the effect our eating has upon the earth?

For ideas on eating low on the food chain, go to www.tryveg. com or www.goveg.com. The PETA website also has a friendly vegetarian section at www.peta.org.

Project 9: Go Solar

When Jimmy Carter was president of the United States back in the 1970s, he put solar panels on the White House. His thought was that it was time for Americans to look for alternative, sustainable energy sources. He believed that America could completely reduce its dependence upon foreign oil by making just a few simple energy choices at the structural level. He tried to convince Americans of the ethical and practical value of alternative energy.

When Ronald Reagan moved in to replace Carter, one of the first actions he took was to have the panels taken down. His thinking was that Americans didn't want to appear weak. He believed that trying to harness energy from the sun suggested that Americans couldn't get the oil they needed from other people's wells. Now, with our country smarting from the price of overseas oil, it suddenly has become fashionable to consider solar energy as a viable option. This time, we hope it sticks.

Individual college students may not be able to make large inroads into establishing solar power usage, but as a collective they can achieve profound results. Arizona State University, the largest university in America, sits in the middle of a desert.[9] But how does the university get its power? Not from the sun, which beats down on the school nearly 12 months out of the year! Universities like to see themselves as centers of innovation, research, technology and rational science. Ho hum!

College students have the energy (pun intended) to confront this exceptional lack of creativity and resourcefulness. We suggest that students and their friends organize a green revolution on their campuses, with the goal of the revolution being nothing less than to influence their university to shift its entire power source to solar energy. It was not so long ago that bold visions of governments and their university engineers collaborated to achieve the installation of massive hydroelectric dam projects and other energy systems. Not that these innovations were sustainable, but at least the innovators showed evidence of will.

Some states, such as Pennsylvania, give consumers the right to choose the source of the energy they are purchasing (solar and wind are among those choices). Energy companies are required to purchase their energy from whatever source the consumer demands. That wonderfully progressive law puts the power of consumption back into the hands of citizens rather than a few powerful corporations. Some universities in Pennsylvania are shifting a percentage of their utilities to green sources.

A green campaign will not succeed overnight, because too many people and corporations benefit from our remaining dependent on unhealthy energy sources. But tomorrow's world does not belong to those corporations—it belongs to today's women and men who have the moral right to steer this ship on a different course. And our hunch is that some students have a large enough vision to rewire an entire campus for that new course!

For more information on the benefits of switching to green power and green power programs, visit www.greenpower.gov or the Environmental Protection Agency's green power link at http://www.epa.gov/greenpower/.

Project 10: Save the Rainforest

It has been estimated that the world's rainforests are being destroyed at the rate of at least 80,000 acres per day.[10] On an annual basis, that's an area roughly the size of Ohio. That's a lot of rainforest.

There is a myth in the West that these lands are destroyed primarily by indigenous people who do slash-and-burn farming. Yet nothing could be farther from the truth. The true culprits are people outside of the rainforest who go there to access mineral resources (such as gold), build pipelines to export oil, set up fruit farms, or clear thousands of acres to graze cattle. These economic enterprises capture the benefits of the local rainforest for the exclusive purpose of exporting products for profit. The local community almost never benefits. The gold and oil that is taken enriches the bottom line of foreign companies, the fruit is exported for sale, and the cattle is used to supply fast-food restaurants in other countries.

The devastation as a result of these practices that is wreaked on the roughly 50 million indigenous people who live in the rainforest is unconscionable.[11] Their health is compromised by the toxic byproducts dumped into their soil, rivers and lakes. Their way of life is destroyed when they are forced to move out of the jungle. Their food supply is threatened as the animals on which they depend for food die as a result of the loss of habitat. When we destroy the rainforest, we are directly destroying them.

Beyond that, of course, is the destruction of the jungle itself—the amazing ecosystem that over thousands of years has been home to the most wonderful and diverse species in the world. Those large basins of trees are the lungs of the earth, capturing immense amounts of carbon dioxide and giving back oxygen. As the forests are cut down, we lose our ability to absorb the large carbon emissions that our modern society produces, and the global climate has been slowly changing as a result. The health of future generations is at risk as we forge ahead with the sensitivity of a bull in a china shop.

How can you help? Several organizations have made it their mission to put large tracts of rainforest into permanent trusts to prevent them from being destroyed in future commercial efforts. One organization, the Eden Conservancy, is preserving a large section of rainforest in Belize as part of a biological corridor that extends through the continent. The idea is to preserve the local integrity of the rainforest and create a permanent corridor that will ensure the survival of endangered species in that region.

To purchase and permanently set aside an acre of rainforest into the Eden Conservancy Trust costs only $200. This is a great idea for group, campus or religious fund-raisers or for holiday gifts and personal donations. When you purchase an acre of rainforest, the Eden Conservancy will send an attractive Certificate of Trust with your name on it to indicate the number of acres that have been saved.

To purchase acreage, contact the Eden Conservancy through the Jaguar Creek environmental center at www.jaguarcreek.org. Or, to learn more about the importance of rainforests and the effects of deforestation, visit www.mongabay.com.

Project 11: Spread the Vision for the Environment

The resources listed in this chapter will help you get a vision for the environment and learn some simple, practical ways to take care of God's creation. Once you understand the major issues of the current global situation, try to share that vision with others. Some ideas that we recommend for spreading the vision for the environment in your church, school or neighborhood include the following:

- **Celebrate Earth Day.** Ask your church's leadership to make Earth Day a part of the annual church calendar so that at least for one day of the year, your fellow church members will focus on global issues. This is a great way to encourage fellow believers to look outside of the walls of the church and take notice of some of the issues that affect our world today. Also, create some posters or informational handouts promoting Earth Day that you can hang up or hand out in visible places on your local campus, at your church or in your community.

- **Join the Parade.** If your town has an Earth Day parade, strongly urge your fellow churchgoers or Christian classmates to join the event as a clear statement that Christians love the creation of their Lord. However, make sure you discourage people from the temptation to show up at the event with placards and slogans that try to "correct" other people's orientation to the environment. Those behaviors will only alienate people from the gospel. Allow this to be a positive time of public cooperation and affirmation.

- **Set up a Booth.** Set up an informational table or booth in your church foyer or on your local college campus. At your table, be prepared to talk to people who are interested in helping the environment and be sure to have some statistics, information and practical suggestions available to promote environment-friendly tactics.

- **Announce Your Plans.** If you want to kick off a "green the city" effort or any of the other activities listed in this chapter, don't be afraid to ask your pastor or your school officials for their advice as to ways that you can get the word out. Your pastor may let you make a brief announcement during your church service to ask for volunteers, and school officials are often glad to support students who take an active interest in their schools and communities.

- **Hold a Seminar.** Get some friends together and hold a Saturday or Sunday afternoon seminar on the environment for those in your church or school who want to learn more about environmental issues.

Organizations

Adbusters
1243 West 7th Avenue
Vancouver, BC
V6H 1B7 Canada
Phone: 604-736-9401
Fax: 604-737-6021
Website: www.adbusters.org

Earth Day Network
1616 P Street NW, Suite 340
Washington, DC 20036
Phone: 202-518-0044
Fax: 202-518-8794
Website: www.earthday.net

Eden Conservancy
(Jaguar Creek Conservancy Center)
P.O. Box 446
Belmopan, Belize
Central America
Phone: 011-501-820-2034
E-mail: jaguarcreek@aol.com
Website: www.jaguarcreek.org

Environmental Defense Fund
257 Park Avenue South
New York, NY 10010
Phone: 212-505-2100
Fax: 212-505-2375
Website: www.environmental
defense.org

National Wildlife Federation
11100 Wildlife Center Drive
Reston, VA 20190
Toll-Free: 1-800-822-9919
Website: www.nwf.org

New American Dream
6930 Carroll Avenue, Suite 900
Takoma Park, MD 20912
Phone: 877-68-DREAM or 301-891-3683
E-mail: newdream@newdream.org
Website: www.newdream.org.

People for the Ethical Treatment
of Animals (PETA)
501 Front Street
Norfolk, VA 23510
Phone: 757-622-PETA
Fax: 757-622-0457
E-mail: info@peta.org
Website: www.peta.org (also
www.goveg.com)

Try Veg
P.O. Box 9773
Washington, DC 20016
Phone: 301-891-2458
E-mail: info@cok.net
Website: www.tryveg.com

World Conservation Union
(International Union of Nature
and Natural Resources)
Rue Mauverney 28
Gland 1196
Switzerland
Phone: 41-22-999-0000
Fax: 41-22-999-0002
Website: webmasteriucn.org

World Wildlife Fund
United States Headquarters
1250 Twenty-Fourth Street, N.W.
P.O. Box 97180
Washington, DC 20090
Phone: 202-293-4800
Website: www.worldwildlife.org

Yellow Bike Coalition
210 East 10th Street
St. Paul, MN 55101
Phone: 651-222-2080
E-mail: ybc@yellowbikes.org
Website: www.yellowbikes.org

Prisoners

BEFRIENDING THE OUTCAST

Sit back for a moment and imagine life behind bars. A home the size of a van—shared with a stranger. No private bath or toilet. Outdoor activities restricted to a rigid routine. Recreation time is limited to prescribed hours in full public scrutiny. There's always a line to use the telephone, and no number for people to call you back. Meals are served cafeteria style. No garage for hobbies, no dog to chase the stick, no kids to swing over the shoulder.

That is the pretty part of the picture.

Now add the fear and loneliness of being completely removed from anyone who cares about you. Add physical harm, which includes beatings and rape. Add the loss of respect and dignity, the inability to provide for your family, and the vulnerability of wondering if a special loved one will meet someone else. Add a prison record to the resumé and the inability to vote again (if incarcerated for a felony)—a loss of the basic right to citizenship. Add the pure impotence of not being able to make anything out of your life.

Some people live this way because of a couple days' experimentation with drugs. Other people live this way because of a joyride in someone else's car or a $50 heist that went awry and left someone dead. Still others live this way because of cold-blooded, premeditated murder.

What does it say about our society that we have lost the patience to ensure the correctional system continues to treat offenders as human beings? That we have lost the desire to separate those who made a one-time judgment error from those who engaged in torture for sport? That we have found it easier to lock people away in a man-made hell than accept the hard work of rehabilitating them?

Christians are uniquely equipped to stand in the gap of justice for our nation's prisoners. We ourselves have not been dealt with according to our sins but have experienced the mercy of Calvary. We received this mercy not because we were reformed, but because we could not reform ourselves. We continue to commit sins against others and God—malice, deceit and immorality—but we continually experience a patient God who guides us back to the right path with the compassion of a perfect loving parent.

Furthermore, as Christians we are able to care about those in prison because we have our own rich heritage of prison life. Our Lord went to prison and stood trial. He was executed. His disciples experienced floggings and persecution. Thousands of first-century Christians were tortured in government prisons (for breaking civil laws), and hundreds of thousands since have died behind bars, far removed from their loved ones. At this very moment, thousands of Christians around the world are in prison awaiting a judge's decision on their future. Their circumstances are no better than the picture of those we painted at the opening of this chapter.

Christians should care about those in prison because our God is just and fair. We know in our hearts that much of the prison system is misguided at best and sinister at worst, and that it goes beyond the boundaries of punishment and rehabilitation. The abuse experienced by many prisoners is a crime against humanity and against God. We should not honestly believe that anyone deserves to live in those conditions.

But it all seems so overwhelming, doesn't it? What can one person do? In fact, there are many things that we as Christians can do to focus our care on both the prisoner and the prison system. It is downright Christian to love the prisoner, and we strongly encourage you to show prisoners God's redeeming love.

Project 1: Support Prisoners' Families

Often, your local church will find ways to support the families of persons in prison, but if you don't know of a local ministry in your area, there are still ways you can help.

As you start to investigate, you'll find that the needs of each family will vary considerably. One family may be struggling with the problem of having a child in juvenile detention. They may be facing tremendous stress as they consider the future of their child and how painful life has become for him or her. Another family may be dealing with both the emotional and material loss of having the primary breadwinner in their household incarcerated. These families may not have enough money to keep up with their mortgage payments or to put food on the table.

There are many ways that you can help families such as these. You can run a toy drive in your community or on your campus and then donate the toys you receive to the children of prisoners. You can write letters to the families of prisoners to offer them encouragement and support. You can donate resources. You can also get a team together to have a time of sharing with the families who have a member in jail.

A ministry called Angel Tree offers a unique way for people to make a difference in the lives of children whose parents have been incarcerated. Angel Tree is a program run by Prison Fellowship Ministries that seeks to bless the children of prisoners in various ways. One branch of the ministry, Angel Tree Christmas, allows incarcerated mothers and fathers to sign up to have a church volunteer deliver gifts to their children at Christmastime. The volunteers buy new and unwrapped presents and give them to their local Angel Tree ministry (see www.angeltree.org for locations). The presents are then delivered to the prisoners' children in their parent's name. This is one effective way to help a child of a prisoner and make him or her feel special, even though a parent may be absent.

Another branch of the ministry, Angel Tree Camping, gives the children the opportunity to attend various summer camps. The kids participate in all the typical events of a summer camp—games, swimming, arts and crafts, campfire sing-alongs—and also learn about Christ in the process. The costs to send the children to the camps are typically covered by participating churches and a special fund sponsored by Prison Fellowship Ministries.

Angel Tree Mentoring provides yet another way for those in the Church to get actively involved in the lives of prisoners' children. In this ministry, Prison Fellowship Ministries works with local churches to match children of prisoners with Christian mentors who want to make a difference in these young people's lives. Prison Fellowship Ministries also provides the resources, training and ongoing support to help in this effort. Through the Angel Tree Mentoring program, the children of prisoners are given the opportunity to have a solid Christian role model in their life and learn firsthand that Christ truly loves them and cares for them.

Check out the Angel Tree Ministries website at www.angeltree.org for more information on how you can get involved in any one of these ministries.

Project 2: Restore Humanity

More than two million Americans live behind bars.[1] That's approximately two times the population of Montana.

No nation in the world has a higher percentage of prisoners per capita than the United States: For every 100,000 Americans, 700 are in prison (Russia comes in second at 665 prisoners per 100,000 people and the Cayman Islands are third at 600 prisoners per 100,000).[2] Yet perhaps the most disturbing fact of American prisons is the fact that according to the U.S. Department of Justice, African-American males are incarcerated at a rate of 4,848 per 100,000, while incarceration of white males is at a rate of 705 per 100,000. Another way of saying this is that an African-American male is seven times more likely to be imprisoned than a white American male.[3] African-Americans comprise 12 percent of the total U.S. population, but they make up 44 percent of the total prison population.[4]

In surveys about police abuse that we conduct in classrooms, we always find that the African-American males are filled with fear when they are pulled over by a trooper, whereas the white American males just tend to be angry that they got caught. White American males don't fear the likelihood of prison, but African-American males do, because statistically it is a likely outcome for them.

It's not easy to make the case that prisons are a good solution to public crime. Although there is little doubt for the need to protect the public from those who would cause harm and to establish penalties for crimes committed, there is little case to make for the model of shutting millions of people away behind bars and stripping them of their dignity, human rights and safety. It's appalling to us when we travel across campuses to hear how easily some students are able to push aside a prisoner as being a nonperson. "They deserve what they are getting!" "They should never have broken the law!" "You should not have any rights if you are behind bars!"

Do we really believe that prisoners automatically deserve whatever happens to them while they are incarcerated? Do we honestly think that our system is fair to African-Americans? It's important to ask these and other questions. Why? Because prisons by and large create more problems than they solve. Young people learn the world of crime and drugs, and thousands become victims of rape and abuse while locked behind the walls of those caged cities. Recent investigations by Congress have revealed shocking stories of sexual slavery and torture. Of course, none of this is new to the former inmates who have tried for years to get the truth out—but who trusts an ex-con, right?

America's prison system is in need of complete reform. One way that you can help to raise awareness of this issue is to work with others in your community to find out the statistics on what kinds of people are being incarcerated, for what reasons, and for how long. (If you are a student, this would make an excellent research project for one of your classes.) You could also help organize public-consciousness-raising rallies on the campus of your school or in your community to draw attention to some of the problems that you uncover regarding the prison system.

To learn more about the prison system from a human rights point of view, go to the website of Human Rights Watch, a non-profit activist organization that stands on the side of those who have been denied their humanity. They cover a multitude of human-rights issues at home and abroad. Check out their website at www.hrw.org and follow the links to "Prison Issues."

Project 3: Give to a Prisoner

We know a church in Southern California that thought big when they decided to ask the question, "What can we give to prisoners this Christmas?"

As the members of the church brainstormed various possibilities, they got the nutty idea that they should do something for *every* prisoner in Chino State Penitentiary. "What's so big about that?" you might ask. Well, Chino has 17,000 inmates—more than the average number of students that attend a particular university. And that church had approximately 2,500 members at the time.

Here is what they did: In the month preceding Christmas, church members began to bake cookies by the dozens. Home ovens and the church's commercial ovens went into full-time use. The children at the church's school made hundreds of small gifts. The adults and parents wrote cards of greeting—not just signed notes, but handwritten sit-down-and-read-this letters. The church also implemented a fund drive to purchase modern-language Bibles for the inmates. On Christmas day, the prison distributed 17,000 *dozen* homemade cookies, 17,000 handmade crafts, 17,000 personal letters and 17,000 Bibles. Now that is a big labor of love!

You may not be able to write 17,000 letters or bake 17,000-dozen cookies, but you can certainly give to a prisoner in some way. You might even want to get your fellow students or church members involved in coming up with some ways to brighten a prisoner's day.

One idea is to gather a group of friends together from your youth group or college group, pick a local juvenile detention facility, and then brainstorm several ways you might be able to bless the young people incarcerated there. Call the officials at the facility to find out what kind of gifts would be appropriate and how many young people live there. Then come up with a plan and aim high!

This can serve as an excellent way to directly bless the life of someone behind bars and demonstrate the love of Christ. However, it is important that you approach this project with wisdom, caution and care—especially if you're a student. Be sure to work through an agency or organization such as Prison Fellowship to keep any donations or contact with inmates safe, simple and appropriate.

Project 4: Bring Persecution to Light

We will go on record as saying that the best logo ever designed is Amnesty International's logo depicting a humble, lit candle wrapped with barbed wire.

Amnesty International began back in the early 1960s when a British lawyer read a small news clip about two Portuguese students who were given a seven-year prison sentence for the crime of raising their glasses in a toast to freedom. From the government's point of view, the students were a threat to national security and needed to be locked away. The British lawyer had no grand plans for founding an international organization, just a desire to make the case of these two students public. He hoped that forced accountability would cause the government to back down and honor these students' human rights. So, on May 28, 1961, he wrote a letter to the London *Observer* asking readers to write letters in support of the students.[5] Since that time, Amnesty International has grown into an organization of 1.8 million members in more than 150 countries.

The work of Amnesty International is to tirelessly document the abuse of prisoners, raise public awareness around specific cases, and then lobby (with the help of its large membership) to convince governments to stop the abuse. Amnesty International has received the Nobel Prize for its work and has been recognized by human rights organizations around the world as being a true light in the darkness. They have been the singular source of hope for countless human beings who otherwise would have been thrown away by those in power.

Not surprisingly, Amnesty has reaped the ire of governments as diverse as China and the United States. The organization's policy of not aligning with any particular government has led them to issue reports on prisoners ranging from remote villages in Asia to U.S. prisons in Iraq and from communist-styled governments to democracies. Most of the prisoners who are brought to the world's attention by Amnesty International's efforts are political prisoners—those incarcerated because their voice, opinions or ideas conflict with the opinions and ideas of those who are in authority. In today's climate of fear, governments around the world are quickly imprisoning individuals who oppose them simply by branding them terrorist suspects. Amnesty International works to bring honesty to legal proceedings and freedom to the captives.

There are several ways that you can assist in Amnesty International's mission. Perhaps the most common way to help is to commit to a letter-writing campaign that is focused on a particular political prisoner. Amnesty International provides the data on the prisoner, as well as the names and addresses of the key persons in government to whom to write when requesting the prisoner's release. (A number of the political prisoners that Amnesty International supports can be found on the organization's website under the "Act Now" link.) You could make this a fun activity by ordering in pizza and working with other friends or fellow students on this project for an evening. Amnesty International also has plenty of material for students who want to host booths and do some general consciousness-raising on campus.

Work to bring to light the situations of people who are being persecuted for having enough principles to speak out on the issues that their communities or governments want to remain hidden. Contact Amnesty International at www.amnesty.org.

Project 5: Write Letters

Many offenders are shipped to prisons far from their families and have no contact with friends for the duration of their sentence. Over time, many of their friends drop away, leaving them feeling empty and alone. Perhaps you could step in to fill that void.

If you have a patient, tender disposition and a love for prayer, you might want to consider sharing the love of Christ and blessing prisoners by writing letters to them. This is an especially good project for people who want to minister in some capacity but cannot expend much energy on work projects or missions trips, so you might want to consider asking friends or people you know at church to also join you in this effort. If they do not feel comfortable writing letters to prisoners themselves, they may at least be willing to commit to praying for those individuals on a regular basis.

As with the other projects involving prisoners, you should approach writing letters to prisoners with wisdom, caution and care. One excellent organization that you and your church could partner with in this effort is Prison Fellowship Ministries' Pen Pal ministry. Similar to the organization's Angel Tree program, the Pen Pal ministry provides a safe and accountable means by which you can correspond with those prisoners who have been isolated from family and friends. Prison Fellowship Ministries provides an informational guide called "Visit Prison in an Envelope" that outlines who should or should not participate in the program and what do when problems—such as attempted scams, romantic overtures, and other manipulations—occur.

If you or your friends choose to correspond with an inmate, make sure that you can make at least a minimal commitment—say, one letter a month. Meet together with your friends and talk about what you hope to do, and then ask everyone to write his or her first letter right there on the spot. As you receive responses from the inmates, pray together as a small group for these people who have to live away from their families and in conditions that are less than dignifying.

Encourage people in your group to offer Bible study materials to the prisoners. Those prisoners who already have a relationship with the Lord will appreciate your sensitivity in helping them grow spiritually. Others who may never have taken a step toward Christ may find the awful life of prison a nudge toward God. *One word of caution*: Your intention should be to love and befriend prisoners, not necessarily to "win their souls" (although that would be great). Prisoners are likely to be turned off if they sense your letters are merely a method of evangelism.

Project 6: Advocate for Change

The idea of advocacy is central to the Christian experience. We even have One who speaks to the Father on our behalf—the Holy Spirit, our own personal advocate. In fact, advocacy is a component of grace: Jesus voluntarily took on our penalty, and now He asks the Judge to release us from the sentence.

We need to right our thinking regarding the prison system. Christians cannot in good conscience ignore the dehumanizing and cruel approach toward offenders that far exceeds our sensibilities of what is just. We need to advocate for prisoners here and around the world.

One way to advocate for change is to link up with an organization called Justice Fellowship, a division of Prison Fellowship Ministries. Justice Fellowship has already done the hard work of researching and compiling data on the major issues and the specific legislation on prison reform. You can simply contact them at www.justice fellowship.org for information on how you, your friends or your church can make a difference and advocate for prisoners in your area or around the world.

Once you have identified an issue, the next step for beginning your advocacy is to write letters to the appropriate people in political office. It might seem like a drop in the bucket, but your letters and your voice truly do make a difference. Of course, if you choose to write a letter to a political official, there are a few guidelines to follow. One website for activists, 20/20 Vision, suggests the following:

- **Make It Personal.** Personal letters from concerned citizens tend to be more influential than those from an expert. Politicians want to know how their policies are affecting their constituents.

- **Put It in Writing.** Don't type out your letter if you can avoid it. A handwritten letter indicates to the receiver that you are a real person. And avoid sending e-mails or faxes—some offices do not give them the same attention as personal letters.

- **Be Brief.** Politicians are busy individuals and won't read a long and rambling letter. Keep your letter brief, clear and focused on the point you are trying to make.

- **Ask for a Response.** Ask the politician to send back a response regarding the issue you raised. This forces him or her to pay attention to the content of your letter and not just send back a general form letter in response. Make sure to put your return address on the letter—an envelope can easily get lost.

- **Be Courteous.** "Reckless words pierce like a sword, but the tongue of the wise brings healing" (Prov. 12:18). Be kind to the person to whom you are writing, even when you disagree with him or her on an issue.[6]

You can also always advocate for prisoners through prayer. Establish regular prayer meetings with a group of friends or church members who care about this issue to pray for the prisoners in your local or regional jails and prisons. You might even want to pray for specific prisoners that are highlighted on the Amnesty International or Justice Fellowship websites.

Project 7: Spread the Vision for Prison Ministry

In Matthew 5:16, Jesus told His followers, "Let your light shine before men, that they may see your good deeds and praise your father in heaven." As the Body of Christ, we need to join together to focus on the issues of injustice in our world today. One of the ways we can do this is by addressing the needs of prisoners and praying for them.

Encourage your pastor to select a particular Sunday on the church calendar to be the day your church focuses on the needs of prisoners. Be persistent, and provide your church's leadership with copies of any important information or resources that you've found in your research. One idea to suggest to your pastor is that he or she plans the Sunday service around the theme of prisoners. If this doesn't work, you can plan a small group, youth group, college group or other smaller gathering around this theme, highlighting some of the biblical passages that call for justice or tell the stories of prisoners. Some possibilities include:

- **Psalms of Prisoners:** A number of the psalms specifically refer to prisoners or captives, including Pss. 68:6; 69:33; 79:11; 102:19-20.

- **Jesus' Words in the Synagogue:** In Luke 4:18-19, Jesus reads the scroll of Isaiah and proclaims, "He has sent me to proclaim freedom for the prisoners and recovery of sight for the blind, to release the oppressed, to proclaim the year of the Lord's favor."

- **Peter's Incarceration:** In Acts 12:1-19, King Herod arrested some of those who belonged to the Early Church, including the apostle James (whom he had beheaded) and Peter. Later, Peter had a miraculous escape when an angel of the Lord set him free.

- **Paul's Incarceration:** Paul was arrested or imprisoned on several occasions. See Acts 16:16-40; 23:12-35; 28:11-16; Rom. 16:7 (with Andronicus and Junias); Eph. 3:1; 4:1; 2 Tim. 1:8.

Suggest to your pastor that all the Sunday School teachers include the biblical call to care for prisoners in that week's lesson. You can also provide a bulletin insert for your church that summarizes the state of prisoners around the world. (Prison Fellowship Ministries and other organizations can provide you with materials.)

Another excellent way to spread the vision for prison ministry is to have your pastor ask the local prison chaplain to do a presentation to the church on how Christians can get involved locally. Or your pastor can ask the family or a relative of a prisoner to share their story and include specific advice on how to care for the families of prisoners. (You can also ask the chaplain or family to come to your small group for a time of sharing.) If your pastor is unable to devote a service to prisoners, he or she may be willing to have a corporate prayer time focusing on prisoners during the service.

Project 8: Get Educated, Then Educate!

The needs of prison ministry are so immense that it is possible to lose heart and feel as if you have to "leave it up to the professionals." Yet as we have demonstrated in this chapter, there are a number of ways that you can get actively involved and make a difference. Perhaps the best way to raise awareness of this often-complex issue is to use the resources listed in this chapter to further educate yourself on the status of prisoners in the world.

If you are a college student, consider taking some time during your Christmas, spring or summer breaks to learn more about prison ministry. If you have friends, acquaintances or people in your church who are interested in this type of service, urge them to join you in leading a program to raise awareness on your campus, write letters for reform, or participate in an internship.

Prison Fellowship Ministries has developed a wide variety of training programs that might be of interest to you, but at the most basic level, they offer summer internships for anyone hoping to make a difference in the world of prison reform. The internships fall in select areas of focus or study, including criminal justice, program management, marketing, research and development, political science, and others. The International Network of Prison Ministries also provides training to churches and individuals who are involved in mentoring inmates when they are released from prison through its MentorCare Ministries division. You can visit the website at www.prisonministry.net/MentorCare.

An ideal way to raise awareness on your campus or at your church is to put together an information table using resources and information from Prison Fellowship Ministries and/or Amnesty International. Get permission from your school or church to put up the table, and then get creative! Write to these organizations, telling them about your plan, and ask for help with brochures, statistical information, resources, and details on letter-writing campaigns. Read up and prepare to tell people about your heart for prison reform or for advocating for prisoners around the world. Stock your table with brochures, sample letters to governments and officials, and resources and books on the subject. You will want to create a simple flyer with some basic information and statistics followed by details on how someone can get involved. Set up your table in a high-traffic area and wait for people to check it out!

If the Lord is putting it on your heart to take some significant steps and to inform your community, friends and neighbors of this area of need, we encourage you to go for it. We do not believe the Church has done enough to reach out to prisoners, so we are enthusiastic when people get excited and want to get involved.

Organizations

20/20 Vision
8403 Colesville Road, Suite 860
Silver Spring, MD 20910
Phone: 301-587-1782
Fax: 301-587-1848
E-mail: vision@2020vision.org
Website: www.2020vision.org

Amnesty International
5 Penn Plaza, 14th floor
New York, NY 10001
Phone: 212-807-8400
Fax: 212-463-9193
E-mail: admin-us@aiusa.org
Website: www.amnestyusa.org

Angel Tree Ministries
44180 Riverside Parkway
Lansdowne, VA 20176
Toll-Free: 800-552-6435
Fax: 703-554-8650
Website: www.angeltree.org

Human Rights Watch
100 Bush Street, Suite 1812
San Francisco, CA 94104
Phone: 415-362-3250
Fax: 415-362-3255
Website: hrwsf@hrw.org

**International Centre for
Prison Studies**
3rd Floor, 26-29 Drury Lane
London, England WC2B 5RL
Phone: 44-0-20-7848-1922
Fax: 44-0-20-7848-1901
E-mail: icps@kcl.ac.uk
Website: www.prisonstudies.org

**International Network of
Prison Ministries**
P.O. Box 4200
Sanford, FL 32772
Fax: 407-323-4336
Website: www.prisonministry.net

Prison Fellowship Ministries
44180 Riverside Parkway
Lansdowne, VA 20176
Toll-Free: 800-552-6435
Fax: 703-554-8650
Website: www.prisonfellowship.org

Prisoner Pen Pal Program
P.O. Box 2205
Ashburn, VA 20146-2205
Toll-Free: 800-497-0122
Website: www.prisonfellowship.org

The Oppressed
UPHOLDING THE DOWNTRODDEN

Christianity has the sense of being foreigners—strangers in a strange land—at its roots. It also has the sense of oppression at its roots. Much of Israel's early literature recalls the days of the Hebrew captivity in Egypt, when God showered extreme favor on the nation by freeing them from the tyrannical rule of Pharaoh. At times when Israel seemed to forget the name of the Lord and drifted from His ordinances, Yahweh reminded them of the days of exile: "[You] were slaves of Pharaoh in Egypt, but the LORD brought [you] out of Egypt with a mighty hand" (Deut. 6:21-22; see also Num. 24:8).

God instructed Israel regularly on the need to help those who were oppressed. The implication was that their future well-being depended on their obedience to this command. "Is not this the kind of fasting I have chosen," the Lord said through the prophet Isaiah, "to loose the chains of injustice and untie the cords of the yoke, to see the oppressed free and break every yoke?" (Isa. 58:6). In a time of frustration when the Lord did not seem to hear the cry of Israel, another prophet asked, "What does the LORD require of you? To act justly and to love mercy and to walk humbly with your God" (Mic. 6:8). Israel understood that God was not entertained by the structure and patterns of worship if it did not lead to them actually doing justice.

In the New Testament, Jesus continued the conversation with Israel's religious leaders. In His famous "Woe to you" speech (see Matt. 23), Jesus chided them for being zealous in their religious practices but without substance in their calling. He told them that their missionary efforts were so off the mark that they produced converts who were "twice as much a son of hell as you are" (v. 15). Jesus said that they had put their focus on issues such as tithing and keeping the Sabbath while neglecting "the more important matters of the law—justice, mercy and faithfulness" (v. 23). He told them that they had been so careful in their filtering of the Law that they managed to strain out a gnat but swallow a camel (see v. 24).

These are not flattering words. Of course, Jesus had the authority to say them.

What would Jesus' words be to us today? Have we "done justice" and attended to the needs of the oppressed? Doing justice is a demanding ministry. It requires us to go beyond our daily spiritual routines and beyond meeting people's immediate needs such as hunger or shelter. Doing justice requires us to look at the systems that cause people's pain and go beneath the surface to change the way the world works.

It is unfortunate that in the past, the Church has not led the way for justice and does not have the reputation for defending the rights of those who are oppressed. In fact, the Church has, historically, tended to side with those who were doing the oppressing. In some cases, the Church has had a strange double standard.

Most Christians in America are aware of the persecution that has occurred over the years to their fellow believers in

China. Many have rightly understood that the government has acted unjustly and have worked to call China to account for its unfair treatment of its citizens. Yet it is much harder for us to turn the spotlight around and question some of our own nation's actions and policies that have resulted in the abuse of various ethnic and minority groups. As a result, we have largely "shrugged off" our nation's policies that have in the past served to support evil governments and oppress others.

Unfortunately, by doing so, we have lost much of our integrity in the view of the world. Our motives have become suspect, for we are always able to point out the speck in the other countries' eyes but unable to acknowledge the log in our own. It happens in this country as well. For instance, at a march for gays and lesbians in the early 1990s held in downtown Philadelphia, scores of Christians showed up to shout slogans of condemnation at the men and women who were quietly making the case that they should have equal rights. Through the din of the shouts, a soft chorus of voices began to grow: "Jesus loves me this I know." The gay marchers were singing about someone who died as an outcast—someone with whom they felt some solidarity. The Christians' response was to increase the volume of their derisive slogans.

Some would argue that the response these examples illustrate is not true of all of us. Certainly, there have been a number of people in the Church—such as Mother Teresa—who have taken a stand for justice and worked to help the needy and oppressed, and movements within the Church—such as the recent Emerging Church movement—have led many Christians to look outside of their own situations to seek ways of actively helping the outcast and downtrodden. Yet we cannot honestly say that the Church has historically been a leader in our society in the ways of compassion.

We have the opportunity in the days ahead to clean the slate, to stand for justice, to counter the prevailing sense that our God condones oppression. We need to feel a strong jealousy for the name of Jesus and set the public record straight. Jesus is not only opposed to oppression; He Himself died an unjust death through a flimflam trial in Jerusalem. Jesus is a friend to the oppressed; therefore, we must work diligently to act justly, love mercy and walk humbly with our God.

Project 1: Tunnel of Oppression

In 2000, a group of students and staff at the State University of New York created a walk-through experience on their campus as a means of pulling students into a discussion regarding the subject of oppression. Called the "Tunnel of Oppression," the exhibit featured a number of rooms in a multiroom set that depicted shocking scenes of genocide, rape, racism and sexism. The props included video footage, skits, posters, sculptures and paintings—most of them created by students.

The students who walked through the series of rooms were profoundly affected by the raw, unedited visuals that they saw. "I'm about to go into the real world," said one student who recently went through the exhibit, "and all those issues are a reality. It really hit home."[1] Since that first show at the State University of New York, the idea has spread to dozens of campuses across the United States.

The Tunnel of Oppression is a great way for any campus to create an annual student-body event that draws on the diversity of the campus. Theater, painting, videography, sociology, justice studies, political science and sculpture are just a few of the disciplines that come together to make this idea successful. Students can choose the subjects that are most meaningful to them (there is no coordinated national agenda), and those ideas can often be related to local events (for example, border states could take on the question of illegal refugees).

For the Tunnel of Oppression to be successful, it has to be extremely creative, polemical and confronting. The event is meant to provoke a reaction from students, stir up public debate and, ultimately, mobilize students for action. Due to the nature of the material presented, the exhibit sometimes brings up old wounds from people's past (rape, assault, abuse), so organizers have found it helpful to provide counseling or refer services at the end of the Tunnel experience. The counselors enable the students to discuss their impressions of what they are feeling, how those impressions relate to real life, and talk about ways to end oppression. Some universities also put up display booths at the end of the Tunnel of Oppression as a resource center for people who would like to put some "feet" to the Tunnel experience.

Hosting a Tunnel of Oppression is a massive undertaking. Most colleges that decide to hold the exhibit put together a team of students from various majors several months in advance. The students plan out the various components of the current year's Tunnel and assign each booth or section to a group. Some universities may even provide college credit for the work that goes into designing and running the event.

Several universities view the Tunnel of Oppression as a form of community outreach. We know of one school that brings in hundreds of high school students from social studies classes each year to tour the Tunnel (parents have to sign off on the field trip because of the disturbing and graphic nature of the content). Another university schedules tours in their Tunnel event for several nearby community colleges. Church, mosque and synagogue groups also schedule tours through the Tunnel of Oppression for the purpose of raising social consciousness about certain issues.

For more information regarding the Tunnel of Oppression, check out the features archive of the *New Paltz Oracle*, the official student newspaper of the State University of New York at www. newpaltz.edu/oracle. Or, for creative ideas on how others have put together a Tunnel of Oppression, simply do a search for "Tunnel of Oppression" on the Internet. You'll be amazed at all the universities that have made the Tunnel of Oppression an annual event and shocked by the bold nature of students who are trying to take the veneer of acceptability off the culture of oppression.

Project 2: Stop the Genocide

Every living president has made some kind of assertion about genocide. The basic message is usually, "Never Again!" Yet without the hard work of preventing genocide—or without a commitment to the choices that opposing it necessitates—"never again" is just a romantic and idealistic notion.

"Genocide" is a recent notion. The word itself is less than a century old and came from a man who suffered the eradication of his family in a European pogrom.[2] Our grandparents' generation came from the unthinkable age of Hitler, when six million Jews (along with millions of others, including disabled people, gays, lesbians and gypsies) were murdered to create the leader's vision of creating a pure race of human beings.

Our horror notwithstanding, nations from other parts of the world have followed the example of our German cousins. Since the days of the Holocaust, the terror of genocide has been enacted on the citizens of countries such as Cambodia, Rwanda and Bosnia Herzegovina. While the nations of the world discuss these contemporary tragedies, they have paid minimal interest during the past three years to the genocide occurring in Darfur, Sudan, which has claimed an estimated 400,000 lives.[3] Besides gaining the attention of a few impassioned movie stars, Darfur has mostly been a yawn of a news item that has sustained almost zero public interest or outrage.

Genocide is possible in part because of people's ability to dehumanize and demonize others. When the United States dropped atom bombs on the cities of Hiroshima and Nagasaki—killing an estimated 115,000 to 175,000 civilians in the initial blast alone—the American public was deadened to the horror of the death toll because the Japanese had been portrayed as little more than rats during the war.[4] When the Hutus slaughtered 800,000 Tutsis in Rwanda 10 years ago, they called the Tutsis "cockroaches" and invited the public to exterminate the pests.[5]

There is always some kind of explanation that every country makes about why it has to destroy so many civilians. The trusted partner of genocide is national security: *We are doing this for our own safety.* After all, who would argue with the need for self-defense? Leaders do not tell their citizens that the decision to destroy civilians comes from an evil desire to commit genocide. Quite the opposite: They turn the gruesome act into a righteous cause.

The likelihood of a future in which no government or civilian population agrees to the slaughter of hundreds of thousands of people is probably remote. Nevertheless, we believe that there are ways to slow the tide. To this end, we want to encourage you to take three types of action.

First, decry dehumanizing language whenever and wherever it occurs. Sexist jokes, racist remarks, gay bashing, negative depictions of Arabs or Muslims and slurs against Mexicans are all mechanisms designed to deprive people of a shared humanity. In the early 1900s, a strong tradition in Germany of demonizing Jews made it possible for a struggling Nazi party to gain an economic and political footing. Theological literature allowed for a view of Jews as the people who crucified Christ. Blatant racist language was used in social conversation and jokes and literature were allowed that depicted the Jews as a people worthy of derision. Such a dehumanization of the Jewish people set the framework for the genocide that would eventually occur during the course of the Holocaust. Genocide is the end of a slippery slide that begins with small attacks on a group of humans. It builds over time in a context considered "acceptable" in the current milieu until the group to be destroyed has been completely dehumanized.

A second suggestion is to support legislation in the international community aimed at slowing human rights abuses. A number of countries around the world have agreed to conventions regarding torture, genocide and the abuse of women and children, but in most cases, the United States has been reticent to ratify these conventions.[6] The signal sent to the nations of the world is that Americans value their sovereignty above globally held standards of human rights. This form of thinking is no different from the logic of governments in the past that have committed genocide. Sovereignty always mattered more to them than outside conventions on abuse.

A final suggestion is for college students to support a growing national campaign to stop the current genocide in Darfur. College students can sponsor campaigns on campuses across the nation to pressure Congress, the White House and local politicians to act *now*. The United States has the ability to declare economic trade between U.S. companies and the Sudan illegal. It has the option of isolating Sudan from international agreements, conventions and gatherings of world bodies until Sudan agrees to end the genocide. Elected officials need to hear from their constituents that Darfur matters.

For more information on the United Nations' Agreement on Human Rights (including the conventions against genocide and torture, on the rights of children and on the elimination of discrimination against women), visit www.hrweb.org/legal/undocs.html. To learn more about the national and international campaigns on ending the genocide in Darfur, visit www.savedarfur.org or www.darfurgenocide.org.

Project 3: Women in Black

Rape is a common weapon of war. For women, the sight of soldiers coming to liberate a city is also the sight of men coming to reap what is considered their time-honored due for fighting a war—sexual relations with the women.

The stories and the statistics are horrific. On every continent of the world in which war occurs, women are raped in their homes and fields as they seek to flee from an approaching army. They are often rounded up and placed into "comfort houses" to serve the soldiers who come home from a day's work in war, ready to force themselves sexually on as many women slaves as they wish.

Reports of such atrocities to the United Nations abound. During the Bosnian Serbian war, a form of ethnic cleansing was engaged in which the "Christian" armies rounded up Muslim women into slave camps and gang-raped them every night. Once the women became pregnant, they were held until they were about eight months along and then sent back to their Muslim communities with signs that proclaimed these women's babies were part Serbian. The notion was to infiltrate the Muslim community with an outside ethnic seed. As many as 50,000 women were gang-raped during that war.[7]

Women in Black is an international network of women founded in 1988 to protest the ravages of war on women. The network's chief approach is for members to hold vigils dressed in black as a form of protest against war and what it does to women. The vigils, for women only, are now held every week in hundreds of cities in more than 30 countries.

What is so remarkable about these vigils is that they are silent. As the Women in Black mission statement states:

> Mere words cannot express the tragedy that wars and hatred bring. We refuse to add to the cacophony of empty statements that are spoken with the best intentions yet may be erased or go unheard under the sound of a passing ambulance or a bomb exploding nearby. Our silence is visible. We invite women to stand with us, reflect about themselves and women who have been raped, tortured or killed in concentration camps, women who have disappeared, whose loved ones have disappeared or have been killed, whose homes have been demolished. We wear black as a symbol of sorrow for all victims of war, for the destruction of people, nature and the fabric of life.[8]

The women who participate in these Women in Black vigils wear long black dresses and black scarves that cover most of their heads. Usually, they will hand out literature to people passing by, explaining their global mission. The vigils are often held in front of government buildings, military recruitment centers, weapons manufacturing centers, and on university campuses.

Any group of women may organize a Women in Black vigil at any time and in any place in the world to protest any act of violence, militarism or war.[9] The vigil would be an obvious opportunity for women from sororities or from Christian organizations on campus to speak out against the atrocities committed against women in war. For more information on how to get involved and set up a vigil, visit the Women in Black website at www.womeninblack.org or www.womeninblack.net.

Project 4: Rally for Rights

One of the most shocking events of the twentieth century was the Holocaust. At the "peak" of Western civilization—that time of heady arrogance during which the countries of the Western world pictured themselves as superior to all other nations—a Western society (Germany and its allies) managed to systematically kill more than six million Jews. By 1945, it seemed that all the progress humankind had achieved through religious discourse and philosophical discussion had been flushed down the toilet. After all, given what had happened in Germany, who could suggest that Western society had found a moral high ground at this point in its history?

On June 26, 1945, representatives from 50 Western nations met in San Francisco to establish a body (known as the United Nations) that would help countries and communities resolve their conflicts peacefully. Three years after forming this organization, the members unanimously adopted a Universal Declaration of Human Rights to formally establish the inalienable rights of people, equally, throughout the world.[10] By signing the Declaration, member nations hoped to forever end the possibility that a country could violate the rights of other human beings or ethnic groups within its borders—as the Nazis had done during World War II.

In some ways, the Declaration was meant to serve as a guide for how people should treat each other—the "golden rule" of loving their neighbors as they love themselves. Since the release of the Declaration, several other covenants and treaties have been issued around the issues of torture; women's and children's rights; social, political and cultural rights; and, not least, the rights of indigenous peoples. While none of these documents can guarantee that people will respect each other (even sacred texts are violated by their devoted followers), they do create a place for clarifying the expectations that exist between communities regarding the honorable treatment of each other. And woven more deeply into those declarations and covenants is a special regard for people who are the most vulnerable—the poorest, the mostly likely to be oppressed.

We think it makes sense to join together with others to celebrate human rights. One way to do this is to schedule public rallies that advance the rights of ethnic minorities, various religious traditions and other groups that have been marginalized by society. In this way, you can help to raise awareness of human rights violations and work to end oppression in our world.

One group that excels in telling the stories of human rights violations is Human Rights Watch. The organization's website is packed with great information, resources and up-to-date news on human rights violations in specific countries around the world and also on specific global issues such as AIDS, children's rights, counterterrorism, international justice, and refugees. You can visit the Human Rights Watch website at www.hrw.org to connect with the organization's campaigns and get ideas on what issues you can address on your campus.

Additionally, you can connect with specific human rights issues that are occurring in your own community. For example, if you live near a border town, there will undoubtedly be concerns in the community about the treatment of illegal aliens. If you live near a Native American reservation, there may be concerns that toxic waste is being dumped into the community's groundwater. Or, if you live near a large agricultural valley, there may be concerns about the people who work long, backbreaking hours out in the fields and who are exposed to chemicals that will damage their organs and shorten their lives.

The bottom line is to look out for those who are the least of society—those who have a small voice, those who are despised, and those who are most likely to be taken advantage of by others in the pursuit of wealth, security and power.

Project 5: Take Back the Night

Pornography and sexual violence. The connection has been made that when we objectify another person's gender, we leave that person open to pure utilization. The humanity of the person disappears when we perceive him or her simply through our personal sense of pleasure or gratification. The pornography industry, which generates billions of dollars in revenue annually, is ultimately financed by women's bodies.[11] But at what cost to their bodies?

Take Back the Night is an organization that seeks to end sexual violence against women. The organization's origins date back to as early as 1877, when women in England sought to bring attention to how dangerous the streets of London were for women at night. In 1976, women in Belgium lined the streets with candles for the first "Reclaim the Night" march, which was held in conjunction with an international conference to draft a convention against violence directed toward women.

The first Take Back the Night march in the United States was held on November 4, 1977, in San Francisco by Women Against Violence and Pornography in Media. Women lit candles and called out the slogan "take back the night" to highlight the idea that the night was being exploited by the sexually explicit commerce of pornography. It was a confusing and brave time for the organization to take a stand. Women were finally staking their claim to sexual freedom in which men did not call the shots, and for some that meant shedding conservative views of sexuality. But sexual freedom was never meant to be equated with sexual exploitation.

Today, Take Back the Night operates in countries throughout the world, hosting candlelight vigils, conferences, rallies and educational workshops to stem the tide of sexualized violence. The organization's website offers resources, connections to other events (both national and international), a means to post your own events to the site, and a list of organizations that offer assistance to victims of sexual violence.

Take Back the Night also has a creative campaign titled "Shatter the Silence," which allows victims of rape, incest and sexual abuse (called "crimes of silence" because of the shame that surrounds these violations) to post their personal stories of abuse. By posting these stories, the organizers hope to help other victims of abuse know they are not alone and, hopefully, to encourage them to report the violations. You can learn more about Take Back the Night at the organization's website, www.takebackthenight.org.

Project 6: Provide a Home

One social-work professor at a private college in California requires her students to spend a weekend on the streets with people who are homeless. Her hope is that her students will begin to acquire a sense of how vulnerable people really are when they live on the streets.

Consider for a moment that you were homeless. Where would you keep your possessions? Where would you go to the bathroom? Where would you make love? How would you keep your children warm during the freezing winter? Where would you get your mail? How would you get cleaned up for a job interview? What would protect you from others while you are asleep?

The homeless have to get creative to survive. Some groups have developed a way of storing their possessions under manhole covers. Some have developed their own policing methods. Yet the vulnerability of the homeless is all too obvious: Many suffer such abuses as being set on fire with gasoline while they sleep, being clubbed to death, or suffering rape and forced prostitution.

There are many reasons why people are homeless, but one is simply the cost of housing. Some people live so close to the edge financially that the loss of a job means eviction. Getting enough money together for first and last month's rent (not to mention the security deposit) becomes almost impossible. Once on the streets, the individuals find it difficult to get a new job, and so the cycle goes.

For too many, this is a downward spiral. Worldwide, the United Nations estimates that more than one billion people have unsafe or inadequate housing.[12] Most often, these are people who have been forced off their arable farming land and have moved to shacks or tenement housing found in large urban settings in search of a new life. Their homes in the urban centers become centers for disease, crime and loss.

One of the simple answers to homelessness and degraded living environments is to provide safe, livable, affordable housing. In recent years, former U.S. president Jimmy Carter has partnered with Habitat for Humanity to lead the way for hundreds of thousands of volunteers to spend their weekends and vacations building homes throughout the United States and in 100 countries throughout the world. Already, Habitat for Humanity has built more than 200,000 houses worldwide, providing homes to more than one million people.[13] The organization often sets up its home-building sprees over college spring break or summer vacation times so that volunteers can build a home from start to finish in one week. Sometimes, at the local level, volunteers will spend their Saturdays over a couple of months to put up a home in their own town.

Without a doubt, Habitat for Humanity has succeeded in taking the politics out of providing homes. In fact, it's common to see both Democrats and Republicans side by side doing what they know makes sense. The United Nations has even designated the first Monday of every October the official international Habitat Day. To find out how to become involved or to volunteer with a house-building project, visit the Habitat for Humanity website at www.habitat.org.

Project 7: Clothesline Project

One out of four women in America will be a victim of sexual violence during her lifetime.[14] For many of these women, secrecy and shame surround the violation.

For women, the college years seem to be the period of life when a high percentage of these violations occur. Many male students use the cover of alcohol and parties to take advantage of women who become vulnerable in those settings. Men often justify date or campus rape through the language of "She asked for it," "It was all in good fun," and other equally horrendous excuses for harming another human being.

One way to extend community and healing to women who have experienced sexual violence is through a public display known as the "Clothesline Project." (It is also an excellent educational opportunity for men.) For this project, volunteers set up a booth in a public, walk-through space on a campus (ideally near the student union building, where high foot traffic is guaranteed), and then hang several temporary clotheslines in the space. With the help of sponsors, volunteers purchase plain T-shirts in a variety of colors (stores such as Kmart have been known to make a donation of tees for this purpose). Each color of T-shirt represents a different kind of sexual violation (for example, rape, incest, battery, murder).

To get the project started, volunteers hang about a dozen of these colored T-shirts on the clothesline. Each shirt has a specific message written on it in color pens or paints. The message is typically about, to or by someone who has been impacted by sexual violence in some form. Some of these messages are epitaphs for lost loved ones, some are words of encouragement for fellow abuse survivors, and others are expressions of emotions regarding the violation. Students on campus are invited to write their own message on a shirt and hang it on the line. Often, the clotheslines are set up in a grid pattern, and after a day or two, an entire "roof" is created on the mall from the shirts that tell the stories of violation. As a kind of hushed sanctuary covers the public space, the extent of sexual violence quickly becomes apparent.

If you decide to have a Clothesline Project at your school, be sure to have several resources available, including: material from local community organizations that work with victims of sexual violence; literature from the local police department regarding the criminal nature of and penalties for sexual violence; and information from campus centers that focus on this social ill that tells people how to connect with their offices.

As an alternative or addition to this project, student groups could set up complementary booths in the same public space. For example, one campus had a couple fraternities host a booth that said in bold letters, "You called it sex, she called it rape." A star football player was invited to join the booth, and male students handed out literature on stamping out campus rape. The students were honest enough to offer up why their parties were often the context for date rape. Another booth had a police officer present who explained how to file a criminal report for date rape. His presence offered a sober statement on the criminal nature of violating women—no matter how it is justified by the perpetrator.

For more ideas and help on how to start your own Clothesline Project, visit The Clothesline Project website at www.clothesline project.org.

Project 8: Human Trafficking

Surely there is a special spot in hell reserved for those who are involved in human trafficking. Just imagine: People actually wake up in the morning to make a profit by snaring fellow human beings and forcing them into a life of slavery.

The idea that slavery is a thing of the past is sadly not true. Today, the industry is thriving, with an estimated 800,000 to 900,000 people forced into slave-style labor and prostitution each year.[15] Because the trade is not conducted in the open (as it was in the early days of our country, when the brazen sale of humans on market squares was a common, government-supported weekend event), today's slaves are much more difficult to locate and to rescue.

Thankfully, most countries in the world today are signatories to conventions that prohibit any form of human trafficking. Laws are now in place to sanction and punish people who make their profits through the enslavement of other human beings. But the problem is still immense.

Economic need is often the condition that paves the way for human trafficking. Every year, hundreds of thousands of people respond to what they believe are economic opportunities in a distant urban center or another country. They venture out on what they expect to be a one-year contract to perform cleaning services or factory work but are lured into a trafficking scheme that relegates some of them to prostitution and others to remote labor environments.

Corrupt police systems around the world also contribute to the problem. There are numerous documented cases of police officers being bribed to pick up people in a supposed raid. Some of these individuals are never booked—they just disappear without a witness or a word. They are shipped to a remote farm or other location, where they live out the rest of their lives in an environment that is entirely foreign to them. Sometimes, they can't even understand the language. All they know is that if they don't do a solid 14-hour day at the place they have been taken, they will be punished. Some raids conducted by human rights group have found workers and prostitutes chained to their beds at nights. A fire in a large apartment complex in Asia revealed dozens of young people who had burned to death because they were shackled at the time of the fire.

One way that you can get involved in the fight against human trafficking is by starting or joining a local or regional campaign run by an organization that advocates for those being trafficked around the world. You can do this on your campus, at your church, or simply among your friends. The goal of your campaign would be to raise the awareness of those around you as to the severity of the problem.

One organization devoted to this work is humantrafficking.org. The organization primarily deals with trafficking issues in Asia and the Pacific, but it also has a U.S. program. The humantrafficking.org website provides various ways to identify people who may be victims of human trafficking, offers advice on how to become an advocate and rescuer of human slaves, lists local and national government offices that could serve as a resource, and suggests current campaigns both locally and globally for action.

Organizations

The Clothesline Project
c/o Carol Chichetto
P.O. Box 654
Brewster, MA 02631
E-mail:
ClotheslineProject@verizon.net
Website: www.clotheslineproject.org

Coalition for International Justice
National Press Building
529 14th St, NW, Suite 1187
Washington, DC 20045
Phone: 202-483-9234
Fax: 202-483-9263
E-mail: coalition@cij.org
Website: www.cij.org

Darfur Genocide
c/o Res Publica
Darfur Advocacy Project
25 Washington Street, 4th Floor
New York, NY 11201
E-mail: information@darfurgeno
cide.org
Website: www.darfurgenocide.org.

Habitat for Humanity International
Partner Service Center
121 Habitat Street
Americus, GA 31709-3498
Phone: 229-924-6935, ext. 2551 or 2552
E-mail: publicinfo@habitat.org
Website: www.habitat.org

Human Rights Watch
350 Fifth Avenue, 34th floor
New York, NY 10118-3299
Phone: 212-290-4700
Fax: 212-736-1300
E-mail: hrwnyc@hrw.org
Website: www.hrw.org

humantrafficking.org
c/o Andrea Bertone, Director
Academy for Educational
Development
Washington, DC
Phone: 202-884-8916
E-mail:
director@humantrafficking.org
Website: www.humantrafficking.org

New Paltz Oracle
The State University of New York at
New Paltz
SUB 417
1 Hawk Drive
New Paltz, NY 12561
Phone: 845-257-3030
Fax: 845-257-3031
E-mail: oracle@newpaltz.edu
Website: www.newpaltz.edu/oracle

Save Darfur Coalition
2120 L Street NW, Suite 600
Washington, DC 20037
Phone: 202-478-6311
Fax: 202-478-6196
E-mail: info@savedarfur.org
Website: www.savedarfur.org

Women in Black
P.O. Box 20554
New York, NY 10021
Phone: 212-560-0905
E-mail: 074182@newschool.edu
Website: www.womeninblack.org and
www.womeninblack.net

Take Back the Night
E-mail: info@takebackthenight.org.
Website: www.takebackthenight.org

The Elderly

HONORING THE WISE

Proverbs speaks of silver hair as the crown of life, the distinguishing mark of wisdom (see Prov. 16:31). Something went awfully wrong between the time when the book of Proverbs was written and our modern society. The pace of these silver-crowned folks is too slow for our fast-paced lifestyles, so we shove them aside. Their presence is a chore, so we leave them in remote homes. They remind us of our own mortality, so we look the other way when they come near. They draw very little respect from our generation. It is as though they should be ashamed to have declined into old age.

But this attitude toward the elderly is utterly foolish! These people bring to us generations of wisdom, stories of global progress and decline, memories of a time before television, cars, airplanes, moon launches and nuclear bombs. They chart for us the childlike steps of nations determined to be modern, of despots grabbing power, of people trying to be free, of frontiers becoming urban centers. They link together the generation of long ago with the generation of today.

Often, our minds and lives are so cluttered with going and getting that we miss it all. Yes, we certainly miss the untapped gold mine in the rocking chair. Yet when we ignore the elderly, we are more than fools—we are coldhearted and callous. After all, what kind of society measures worth by production output? What kind of people gauge value by mobility and dexterity? What kind of nation measures "human" by "returns"? Think about the waning years of the elderly—all the years they have lived now stored up in their frame, all the people they have known, all the cities they have built, all the wars they have fought, all the fields they have planted, all the droughts they have survived, all the children they have birthed (and perhaps buried), all the frontiers they have settled, and all the moments they have experienced that changed the course of the ages.

Many of the elderly remain active and sharp in their final years. Unfortunately, for many more, the waning years are painful and even bitter. They sit to catch their breath, strain to hear the question, squint to see the bird, and are slow to respond when asked, "tea or coffee?" The moments are not so kind on their minds—they confuse yesterday's news with today's soap opera. The sun sets much slower than they recall of old, and children play at war as if there never really was one. And their family pushes them aside to the chair in the corner like some vase Aunt Elda gave them 20 Christmases ago.

It is strange to reflect on how pro-life Christians often claim to be, defending lives that have yet to see a sunrise while discarding those that have seen 1,000 times 30. If the integrity of our pro-life commitment is measured by the scale of honoring the elderly, it is clear that we are not doing so well. In our hectic pace and flagrant clamoring for more, we have missed the gravity and dignity of those so tempered by the ages.

We believe that Christians need to steer society back to giving the elderly the love and respect they deserve. We need to return to the days when silver hair was a crown and when children and adults alike sat at the feet of Grandma and Grandpa to learn from their wisdom. This is a Christian duty, and leaders need to set the course.

Project 1: Go Shopping

One of the biggest challenges for some people as they move into their senior years is loss of mobility. Life can gradually slip into a narrow world defined by apartment walls and a television box. If they do not have family nearby, the day becomes a tragically lonely time.

It's not always easy to know how to merge into the life of people who are shut in. But one very natural point of contact is shopping for food. Elderly people often end up with a diet that resembles the worst of hospital food, frozen foods and microwave meals for no other reason than the difficulties they encounter negotiating traffic and aisles.

To find out how to connect with people who live a mostly shut-in lifestyle, contact your local social services offices or religious group (your church might sponsor a related program). Join with at least two other friends to make a commitment to do a few regular shopping hours per week for a person who is shut in.

Here's how this typically works. First, you and your friends find a person who would love assistance when he or she is shopping. Visit that person for a planning meeting and talk through what he or she likes to purchase, what stores he or she likes to frequent, and what budget he or she needs to work within. Agree on a time for the first shopping trip, and be sure to show up at least five minutes early for the first outing.

Don't take charge of the shopping. Most people relish the chance to make decisions for themselves, sort through the various vegetable options, and compare prices. Your job is to provide a kind of buffer to the pace, crowd and noise. Keep in mind that the shopping trip will take much more time than you are used to and will require building trust with someone who only knows you as a stranger. Be exceptionally patient, stay conversational and don't offer advice!

When you stand in line to purchase the groceries, stay in the background so that the person is the one talking with the checkout staff. Perhaps you can offer to bag the groceries. If the staff talks directly to you, defer to the person who is buying. (One of the negative experiences of growing older is that people start avoiding eye contact and/or conversation with the individual. This shuts in the person even more than he or she already was.)

Be sure when bagging the groceries to ask how the person wants them to be packed. Some folks have 50-plus years of routines that matter to them. Back at the house, when unloading the groceries, be sure to store all the items exactly the way your client wants them stored. Don't become a closet organizer or kitchen remodeler. The person whom you are helping needs to sense your respect and delight in how he or she has set up the home. It can be tempting to do something a little bit more "sensible," but the bottom line is that such help is insensitive.

Over time, you may discover what coupons your client likes to use for shopping. Scour local papers and stores for similar coupons and bring those along for the next shopping outing. It's a dignified way to bring someone's shopping bill down without a handout.

Project 2: Record the Stories

We need to structure times with the elderly that help us, as people, regain our admiration for them. One way that we can do this is to ask the elderly to help assemble our history—to tell the stories of the past that will help us learn how we are connected to the generations that have come before us. Here are a few activities that you could do to accomplish this:

- **Create a Theme Evening.** Ask some of the older folks in your church to describe their homes of old. Involve your friends or small-group members in your church to draw the plan of the house as it is described. List the appliances and utilities that made their homes operate, and then draw a contrasting picture of our current homes. Other themes could include transportation, technology, kids' games or work. The idea is to get the older folks talking and sharing their memories with those in the younger generations.

- **Paint a Picture.** Ask those who have lived in your town or community for many years to tell what it was like "way back when." Ask them to paint a verbal picture of life in the good ol' days. You might even arrange a four-stop virtual tour through the town and have them explain what used to be there. (We recently spoke to someone who remembered when the Los Angeles International Airport was just one small tin shed and a landing strip.)

- **Talk About Family.** Ask the elderly to talk about their family. Plot out their family tree on a blackboard or whiteboard, going as far back as they can remember. Include where they were from, what they did for a living, the names of their children, and so on. You will develop a fascinating sense of being just a few breaths away from famous events, such as World War II.

Don't worry if the event doesn't go absolutely according to plan—the very act of sitting at the feet of the elderly will go beyond any words that you could articulate to demonstrate that you respect and honor them.

Project 3: Work for the Elderly

Many of the elderly in your church and community are probably still living in their own homes. They maintain wonderful gardens, enjoy their hobbies and keep up with the repairs. But it does become more difficult over time to maintain these habits.

Slowly but surely, the elderly must let some things go as the tasks become too difficult and strenuous for them to manage. The oranges on the top branches rot, the hedge does not carry the same square trim, the weeds are equal to the grass, the variety of flowers diminishes. Of course, watching these things slip can be very depressing for them.

Why not pick up some of the slack for the elderly in your community? The idea is simple: Gather a trusted group of people who would like to volunteer for a few hours each week. Starting with the elderly in your church, get the word out through your pastor, leaders or even the bulletin that your volunteer team is ready. Explain that you would like to take on regular routines such as garden care and housecleaning as well as fix-it projects, such as a broken lock, a cracked window or a dripping faucet.

You will probably be able to manage all of these items without much more than word of mouth. However, if the task gets too large, create a way for the elderly to request help. For example, the elderly person could write up requests on index cards, complete with name and phone number, and post them on a bulletin board that is designated expressly for the elderly. The group of volunteers can check the board regularly and take those cards that they will handle. Alternatively, you could have one person in your group be the contact person that the elderly person can call when a situation arises. That person would then be responsible for delegating the tasks to those in the group.

If you find the system is working well and enough energy is going around to expand the idea, consider broadening the program to elderly folk who are not a part of the church. They are not as likely to be attached to a group or club that would offer this kind of help, and it makes a lot of sense that the church would be there to stand in the gap.

Project 4: Reach Out to the Elderly

Chances are your town has a convalescent center where dozens of people do not receive regular visits from family. In our experience, these centers are sensitive to their members and would be more than happy to suggest someone who you could befriend.

A great way to honor the elderly is to enlist a group of friends and volunteers who would be willing to visit people at least once a week and always on the same schedule. Try to find a team that includes a variety of ages—older adults, middle-aged and young people—so that communication can happen at several levels. If you have younger siblings or know some young children, it would be fun to bring them along. Children are especially valuable to the elderly.

It is sad that our society is so uneasy with the vision of growing older that we tend to try and protect our children from those who are advanced in years. We think that we are doing them a favor, but in fact what we are doing is teaching them not to respect their elders and to fear old age. Nor is it fair to the elderly. If you have included children in these kinds of routines, you know the delight they bring—the hugs, the handholding, the laughter, the stories recounting younger years. What a gift! Of course, be sure to first orient your children to the environment.

They may not be prepared for the spontaneous manner of some older folk, who may reach out to hug them. Tell the kids it is okay to hug back.

Some kids will have their first experience with death in this context. We know of kids who insisted on going to the funerals of friends they had made in the convalescent center. Yes, the experience was traumatic, but that is the nature of life. And death is part of life. Learning to grieve in youth is good and fair.

You may even want to include pets in some of your visits. Many convalescent centers actually request this service. Friendly dogs and cats bring back good memories for many people whose last household companion was a pet, and animals love the attention. It's not every day they can receive hugs and strokes for several hours. Check with your center for their specific guidelines. You may discover your town has a special service just for this. In some cities, it is called the "Pet Parade." These organizations provide pets that are trained to give and receive love and affection. You can actually "check out" these pets for a regular routine of visitation.

Project 5: Give to the Elderly

A small farming town in the Northwest has found a wonderful way to involve children in giving to the elderly. The town has one school and one convalescent center. Since many of the school kids have relatives living in the center, the town developed a way to bring these groups closer together.

The lower grades are typical of any school; they do crafts every other day (or so it seems). These crafts serve as a good learning tool in creativity, but unfortunately, they are usually tossed out at the end of the week, if not the end of the day. On special occasions such as Thanksgiving, Christmas and Valentine's Day, the crafts get a little more extravagant, but they too hit the basket before long.

However, this particular school came up with a creative solution: On holidays and other special days, the kids in the lower grades make cards and crafts for the folks in the local convalescent center. The convalescent center is a wonderful sight on these special days, and the elderly truly appreciate the thought.

If your town has a convalescent home, you can follow this little town's lead. Start by visiting the center to get to know some of the folks who live there. Bring your friends. If you feel really ambitious, get your church's preschool director involved and ask if he or she would be willing to participate by having all the preschoolers make cards for the elderly. Also ask some of your area preschools to participate and, if possible, let the kids deliver the cards and crafts themselves. The reaction from the folks will be that much greater!

Organizations

American Association of Retired Persons
601 E Street NW
Washington, DC 20049
Toll-Free: 1-888-687-2277
Website: www.aarp.org

National Association of Area Agencies on Aging
1730 Rhode Island Avenue NW, Suite 1200
Washington, DC 20036
Phone: 202-872-0888
Fax: 202-872-0057
Website: www.n4a.org

National Meals on Wheels
203 South Union Street
Alexandria, VA 22314
Phone: 703-548-5558
Fax: 703-548-8024
Website: www.mowaa.org

United Way of America
701 N. Fairfax Street
Alexandria, VA 22314
Website: www.national.unitedway.org

The Sick and Disabled

SERVING THE AFFLICTED

Think back to the days when you were just a child in Sunday School or to when you first heard stories about Jesus. It probably seemed at the time as if half of all the stories you heard about Jesus were His encounters with the sick or the disabled: the woman who touches His gown and is healed (see Luke 8:40-56); the blind men beside the road who called out to Jesus for healing (see Matt. 20:29-34); the Roman leader pleading for his daughter's life with great faith (see Luke 7:1-10); the paralyzed man being lowered through the roof to see Jesus (see Mark 2: 1-12); the raising of Lazarus from the dead (see John 11:38-44).

Jesus could not pass up a sick person. The famous missionary verse "Ask the Lord of the harvest, therefore, to send out workers into his harvest field" (Matt. 9:38) is actually the prayer Christ prayed after going through several towns and villages healing "every disease and sickness" (v. 35). Jesus tells us that one way to recognize His disciples is by their behavior.

Sickness and disability come at several levels. It can simply be a temporary nuisance or it can permanently immobilize a person. The Church should be particularly concerned about people whose lives are permanently altered due to health problems. When people lose their health, they constantly feel a deficit. Something has been taken from them. They cannot muster up the energy to do their work, or perform simple duties that before were done so easily, or laugh without wincing from the pain.

Sometimes, sickness brings about a change in relationships. People are not sure how to act around sick people, so they avoid them. They are not a natural pick anymore to hang out with on a Friday night. They might experience deep depression or a sense of uselessness. To them, it may seem as though their dignity disappeared with their health.

When Europe experienced the Black Plague, as many as one-third of all people on that continent died. An unusually large percentage of those individuals were Christians. Historians tell us that the apparent reason for this was because while citizens were packing their goods and fleeing to other towns in order to avoid the Plague, Christians stayed behind to care for the sick. This was not a form of simple charity. It was an invitation to death—contact with the Plague was fatal. So Christians died in large numbers as they ushered the sick into their eternal reward. That kind of commitment is astounding. Would Christians today do the same? Could we find it within ourselves to pay the same price? That is a tough question to answer. Thank God few of us will have to face that dilemma. The modern-day challenge to care for the sick is not so costly.

The Old Testament offers a picture of the day when the lame will throw aside their crutches and run at full pace to the city of Zion (see Isa. 35). There will be great laughter and tears of joy, for in that day we shall all be made fully whole—body, soul and spirit. The night of struggle and the lifetime of limping will be over. The redemption will be final and complete. The story belongs to all of us.

We are wrong to push aside those with physical disabilities and relegate them to a lesser place in the order of life and church. Indeed, it may be more appropriate to assign people with physical disabilities a place of honor in this life—slightly higher than the rest of us. They more perfectly reflect Israel's night of struggle; they more honestly exhibit the truth regarding the human condition. It is through them that we are taught that we cannot have Christ without the cross.

As Christians and as people, we must demonstrate the way of compassion today. This suggests that we must take on the pain and cries of those who live with chronic illness or disability. It means not avoiding those we would rather not be around. It means serving the people even when a cost is involved.

Project 1: Show Compassion to Modern Lepers

"Unclean! Unclean! Unclean!" In Jesus' time, shouts and ringing bells warned people that lepers were approaching. "Clear the way! Don't get close enough to touch them or you yourself may become infected! It will eat your body, and you will die before your days are meant to end!" Yet Jesus held the hands of lepers. He touched them, soothed them and comforted them.

The most recent example of this model of compassion came from an outstanding Albanian woman who emulated Jesus' model closely. Around the world, she is still admired today— almost even worshiped. When she was alive, wherever she traveled, people rushed to her and stretched to touch her hand, crying out "Mama! Mama!"

Mother Teresa, friend of the world. Why did she garner so much love and admiration? She was a friend to the leper. She gave up her citizenship to become a permanent resident of India and made her life mission to care for the "least of these." Calcutta, a giant city that portrays so perfectly the human tragedy, became home to the Mother of Mercy. Sounds a bit like Jesus, doesn't it?

And what about the latest version of leprosy—AIDS? The United Nations estimates that more than 38 million people in the world today suffer from this deadly disease.[1] Nearly 3 million people died last year from AIDS complications, and of those, 500,000 were children.[2] In some regions of the world, entire villages have been decimated in places where parents, teachers, administrators and commerce leaders succumbed to the disease.

When the first AIDS cases were recorded a little more than two decades ago, its origins were attributed mostly to the homosexual community. Like a prairie wild fire in the wind, the idea of a "gay disease" was soon solidified in the public mind. Preachers proclaimed God's judgment on sinners while politicians shied away from quarantine measures that might have interrupted the phenomenal growth of the epidemic. The initial national and global response to the AIDS outbreak will not go down as a high point in our history.

More recently, governments experiencing the decimation of their nations' economies and communities at the hands of the disease have made controlling the spread of AIDS a top priority in their countries. The United Nations has coordinated a massive public campaign, UNAIDS, to seek ways of overcoming AIDS through medical intervention, education and donor-country support. Celebrities such as Irish rocker Bono, former South African political prisoner Nelson Mandela, former U.S. president Bill Clinton and billionaire Bill Gates have fought tirelessly to keep attention focused on the AIDS problem. Given the gay bashing that marked AIDS from the outset, it has taken this extraordinary coming together of larger-than-life human beings to convince the public to stay focused on the disease.

As celebrities put AIDS on the conscience of those in the Western world, a grassroots movement emerged in the Third World to fight against pharmaceutical companies that were profiting massively from the sale of AIDS drugs in the West while people in poorer countries were dying because they could not afford those same drugs. The largest grassroots organization in Africa, Treatment Action Campaign (TAC), sued a dozen pharmaceutical companies while simultaneously suing the South African government for not meeting its constitutional obligation to provide medical care to the poor. The campaign was joined by India and Brazil, both of which threatened to defy the drug patents in order to meet the demand of a larger ethical issue—human survival. TAC won on both fronts, and now life-saving drugs are beginning to trickle down to the poor.

There are several actions you can take to join the effort to eradicate AIDS worldwide and lessen the burdens of those who live with it. The first is to identify positively with people who suffer with AIDS. A group of churches in Africa sponsor an annual walk in which everyone from the church wears a bold T-shirt that states "I'm HIV Positive." It's a nice way of saying that everyone is impacted by AIDS in some way and that it is not as important to separate out those who are infected as it is to find ways to support one another in the struggle against the disease. The red AIDS pin has become a universal symbol of resolve and identity, and is an easy and effective way to always keep AIDS in the public eye.

Another idea is to check with your local health-services organizations to find out ways to help when it comes to the AIDS epidemic. For example, many organizations train volunteers to work in hospices that serve as a final home for people with AIDS. Such volunteers often find that they bring friendship and a sense of community to people who have been cut off from families who either disapprove of them or are afraid of them. These hospice workers often end up helping families say goodbye to their loved ones in a way that is dignified, reconciling and healing to the spirit.

You can also link up with the annual World AIDS Day (which always falls on the first day of December) by joining rallies or marches to link arms with other people who are devoted to overcoming both the prejudice against people who are HIV positive and the challenges of the disease itself. For other ideas and resources, visit the UNAIDS website at www.unaids.org. Also check out Bono's organization, www.data.org, a contemporary site devoted to AIDS and trade issues in Africa.

Project 2: Bridge the Gulf

Many people feel uncomfortable around those with disabilities. Our quest for immortality, our culture's fixation with the perfect body, and high society's club of the beautiful people are all barriers to the gospel fact that God created us all in love and dignity. We all carry the full measure of His image in us. The Church needs to stand against the lie that handicapped people are lesser beings and begin to reflect the truth of God's creation.

Christians need to call their church communities to bridge the gulf that separates people in our society according to physical capabilities. Several ways to do this include:

- **Be Accessible.** Ensure that your church meets the current federal standards under the American Disabilities Act for people who have physical limitations—including ramps, special seating areas and rest rooms that are wheelchair accessible.[3]

- **Provide Transportation.** Consider volunteering or get a team of people together who can provide regular transportation and other services for those who require assistance in your community.

- **Include the Disabled.** Get the word out that you want to bring the disabled into the regular life of the church because your church needs them. Invite those who are new to your church to join a small group or regular community gathering, and offer to provide transportation.

You might also want to talk with your pastor or elders at your church to determine other ways that those with disabilities can be included in the church service. Perhaps people with disabilities could regularly lead a portion of the service.

Project 3: Establish a SickNet

Sometimes we are caught off guard by a friend's account of what it was like to be sick for the previous month—the loneliness, isolation, depression, lost income, stacked-up work. Usually, our response is, "Oh, I wish I had known!"

Where do people turn when they need help? Who is ready to give extra help to make their illness a little more tolerable? Who is there to take care of the details that cannot afford to slip? Some people feel awkward depending on others, fearing that they will be a burden. Yet most people are more than willing to lend a hand—if only they knew who needed help.

A SickNet is a simple system that you can employ to make sure people who are sick do not go unnoticed. Here's how the system works: First, recruit a team of volunteers from your church or school. This group of volunteers needs to be willing to sign up for a weekly commitment (or as needs arise) and perform simple tasks to relieve the sick person's burden: cook a meal or two, spend an hour cleaning the house, run a few errands. It would also be helpful to find a couple of people who would like to take the duty of visiting the sick specifically to pray for them.

Next, if someone gets sick, he or she calls the designated SickNet coordinator of the week. The coordinator finds out what the needs are and then contacts people from the roster of volunteers to help meet the specific need. The sick person's name may also be added to that week's prayer chain or prayer list.

Ask members of your team to be on the lookout for neighbors, coworkers or acquaintances who are dealing with physical illnesses or limitations. Emphasize that this program is for *everyone*, not just for close friends or church members. Imagine the impact when a sick mother (who is not a church member) receives a hot meal to feed herself and her three kids. What a statement of love and compassion!

A SickNet will provide you with a wonderful opportunity to tangibly express God's love to those in need. Over time, you may find that you are now in touch with dozens of people who have little history with the Church or with Christ. These kinds of opportunities are wonderful for sharing God's love. The idea is just to be sure you are mentally and physically prepared for a much larger scope of caring than for just a few errands and meals.

Project 4: Support the Families of the Disabled

Sick and disabled people need help, but so do their family members. One of life's sad statistics is the impact of serious illness and disabilities on families. Only 25 percent of marriages survive an illness in which one of the partners is chronically ill, bedridden or immobilized for a protracted period of time (the current national divorce rate is 50 percent).[4]

Divorce rates are also much higher in households in which one or both spouses are disabled. In a 1997 survey conducted by Louis Harris and Associates, 13 percent of those surveyed were divorced, as compared with 11 percent in 1994 and 9 percent in 1984.[5] The stress upon the other spouse to survive financially, manage the household affairs, raise the children and plan for the future is apparently too much. Whereas home used to be that place of shelter, relaxation and rest, now it is an emotional and physical drain.

It is not our place to judge people who cannot survive these circumstances. But it is our place, as Christians, to ask what we can do to support these stressed-out families. One suggestion is to look for qualified volunteers in your church who can attach themselves to families who attend your church and actively search out ways to be useful and supportive to them. Volunteers can help with housecleaning, doctor visits, shopping and yard work to free up the spouse for essential family activities such as playing with the kids, attending to the sick or disabled partner, getting away for some rest time, or going to favorite events. These are the most important elements of family life—and are always the first to go when a crisis hits.

As you branch out to other people in the community, take referrals from church members who want to be involved in supporting their neighbors who may have this need. Encourage the creation of a team around each family. This would ensure a much more consistent style of service and would help prevent burnout for the care providers.

Project 5: Help Find Jobs for the Disabled

In the United States, approximately 70 percent of those with disabilities are unemployed.[6]

Perhaps you know Christians in your church or community who own a business and can help. Hopefully, they have adopted a "Kingdom perspective" of their companies and want to use them for God's glory. It may be possible for these entrepreneurs to employ some of the handicapped people that you know.

This is not to say that these companies should create charity positions for the disabled—that would be demeaning. However, you might want to propose to these business owners that they look for specific slots in their organizations that could be filled by people who have disabilities. For instance, many grocery store chains have begun hiring disabled individuals to bag groceries or collect shopping carts in the parking lot. Other companies have hired disabled individuals to perform certain office functions or provide janitorial services. The Bobby Dodd Institute, located in Atlanta, Georgia, manages a switchboard at a local hospital and hires vision-impaired individuals as telephone operators.[7]

Given the difficulty disabled individuals have in obtaining work, any time it is possible, these slots should be reserved for them. This is an area in which Christian-led companies should be taking the lead. Wouldn't it be great if the business community and the news media rushed to try to figure out why these businesses insist on such a practice and still make a good profit?

One other idea for enterprising young leaders is to invite some key businesspersons and disabled people together for a meeting. Open the discussion by asking each of them the question: Do you suppose it is possible for all of us in this room to create a brand-new business together that would provide a valuable service to our community, employ an unusually large percentage of disabled people, and turn a good profit? The outcome might surprise everyone.

Project 6: Go with the Disabled

One of our fondest memories is of racing through the slums of Mexico City with Tom Brewster. A quadriplegic due to a swimming accident, Tom put most of us to shame with his energy and vision for life. He and his wife, Betty Sue, founded a revolutionary school of language learning that is relationally based versus academic. Tom insisted that language is not a barrier to overcome but a gift that can link us to people of other cultures. He modeled his theory.

It was not easy to keep up with Tom in the slums as he negotiated ruts and rocks in the outlying districts of Mexico City. He was there to teach us how to build relationships with people across cultures, and we have not forgotten his remarkable ability to make friends with all sorts of people. Tom is with Jesus now. His body finally gave in to the deterioration caused by organ failure. He is probably still arguing with Jesus for taking him home too soon. He had much to explore yet and all kinds of people to meet.

The suggestion for this project is based on our loving memory of Tom: If you are going on a trip or even leading a project yourself, make an effort to include people with disabilities. Involve them in the planning process, both for their unique ministry ideas and their understanding of how to accommodate certain disabilities. If possible, also bring them along on the actual trip. You will be amazed at how much they will contribute to your team—and they will learn from the trip just like everyone else you bring along. Your trip will be richer, and your team will look a little more like the Kingdom.

Project 7: Give to the Sick and the Disabled

As mentioned previously, people who are sick are often hesitant to ask for help, even when they are connected to a caring church or community. That response is understandable: They want to preserve their dignity and do not want to feel like a burden.

One church in Chicago has learned to be sensitive to this situation as it concerns the sick in its congregation. The pastor announced a special meeting and invited members who were willing to give a few hours a month for friends and neighbors who were sick. He encouraged each person to show up with crayons, colored pens, scissors and tape. When the volunteers arrived, the pastor stood at a blackboard and asked members to shout out things they wished they could ask people to do for them when they were sick. The members came up with a list that included mowing the lawn, running errands, cooking a meal and taking the kids to their sports practices.

The pastor then asked everyone to think through 12 activities they would be willing to do throughout the year for someone else who was sick—one activity a month. Each volunteer made up 12 special coupons on poster paper, with each coupon describing a specific service they would be happy to perform, and listed their name and phone number on the paper. All of the coupons were collected, shuffled and arranged into packets of 12 (each volunteer appeared no more than once in each packet). Members made colorful envelopes for each of the coupon sets and included the church's phone number and address on the packets.

As the church received calls regarding people who were experiencing serious illnesses, volunteers sent one of these packets to be delivered by the regular visitation team that was already in place. At the end of the visit, the team handed the packet over to the sick person as a gift from the church. The volunteers said that they found the unexpected phone calls to redeem coupons a refreshing break from the normal routine of the month, and it did not seem burdensome because the services were varied and infrequent. The idea has grown to the point that there are now many, many packets in the church office ready to be used.

Taking action for the disabled could be just as easy, if not exactly the same. Take some initiative (with the permission or even participation of your church's leadership) and call a meeting with the disabled members in your church. Ask them, "How can we help you? Are there certain tasks members of our church could perform to help you?" Write the list on a chalkboard and then brainstorm together a system that is both dignified and practical. We know of one group of people at a church that recruited several members to be available to help disabled members. When these needs were called in to the church office, they were simply forwarded to the volunteers, who coordinated to meet the needs. However you go about this, keep in mind that it always needs to occur in the spirit of equality and dignity. Every one of us depends on others—the mechanic, doctor, teacher, counselor—for certain needs. We are simply extending that notion into the Body.

In your own community or church, you might be able to replicate these plans exactly or tweak them slightly to fit your situation. And we encourage churches not to confine these services to the members of their congregation. Our mandate calls us to always look outside our own circle. Seek out people beyond your church who could use your help.

Organizations

**Bill and Melinda Gates
Foundation**
P.O. Box 23350
Seattle, WA 98102
Phone: 206-709-3100
E-mail: info@gatesfoundation.org
Website: www.gatesfoundation.org

**Career Opportunities for Students
with Disabilities**
100 Dunford Hall
Knoxville, TN 37996
Phone: 865-974-7148
Fax: 865-974-6497
E-mail: info@cosdonline.org
Website: www.cosdonline.org

DATA
1400 Eye Street NW, Suite 1125
Washington, DC 20005
Phone: 202-639-8010
Website: www.data.org

**Health Ministries
Association, Inc.**
295 West Crossville Road, Suite 130
Roswell, GA 30075
Phone: 770-640-9955
Toll-Free: 800-280-9919
Fax: 770-640-1095
Website: www.hmassoc.org

Joni and Friends Ministries
P.O. Box 3333
Agoura Hills, CA 91301
Phone: 800-523-5777
Website: www.Joniandfriends.org

L'Arche USA
P.O. Box 5034
Bradford, MA 01835
Phone: 978-374-6928

E-mail: office@larcheirenicon.org
Website: www.larcheusa.org

National AIDS Trust
(World Aids Day)
New City Cloisters
196 Old Street
London, EC1V 9FR
England
Phone: (44) 020-7814-6767
Fax: (44) 020-7216-0111
E-mail: info@nat.org.uk
Website: www.worldaidsday.org

Nelson Mandela Foundation
Private Bag X 70 000
Houghton 2041
South Africa
Phone: (27) 11-728-1000
Fax: (27) 11-728-1111
E-mail: nmf@nelsonmandela.org
Website: www.nelsonmandela.org

Nurses Christian Fellowship
P.O. Box 7895
Madison, WI 53707
Phone: 608-443-3722
E-mail: ncf@intervarsity.org
Website: ncf.intervarsity.org

Postulation of Mother Teresa
2498 Roll Drive PMB 733
San Diego, CA 92154
Phone: 664-621-3763
E-mail: post@motherteresacause.info
Website:
www.motherteresacause.info

Treatment Action Campaign
34 Main Road
Muizenberg 7945
South Africa

Phone: (27) 21-788-3507
Fax: (27) 21-788-3726
E-mail: info@tac.org.za
Website: www.tac.org.za

UNAIDS
UNAIDS Secretariat
20 Avenue Appia
CH-1211 Geneva 27
Switzerland
Phone: (41) 22-791-3666
Fax: (41) 22-791-4187
E-mail: unaids@unaids.org
Website: www.unaids.org

United States Access Board
1331 F Street, NW, Suite 1000
Washington, DC 20004-1111
Phone: 202-272-0080
Toll-Free: 800-872-2253
Fax: 202-272-0081
E-mail: info@access-board.gov
Website: www.access-board.gov

**United States Government
Disability Info**
Phone: 800-333-4636
E-mail: disabilityinfo@dol.gov
Website: www.disabilityinfo.gov

William J. Clinton Foundation
55 West 125th Street
New York, NY 10027
Website: www.clintonfoundation.org

Immigrants

HELPING THOSE NEW TO OUR LAND

Much of the recorded history of our faith concerns people who were foreigners. Abraham was called by God to leave his homeland and go to a place God would show him (see Gen. 12). There, among strangers, he set up his new home. His grandson, Jacob, worked 14 years for his Uncle Laban in a distant land before again settling down in his home place. Once he returned, he lost his favorite son, Joseph, to the schemes of his wicked sons (see Gen. 29,31,37).

Joseph grew up as a foreigner in Pharaoh's prisons and then in his court. A drought forced Joseph's brothers to join him (see Gen. 46:6), and in time, they became the despised and enslaved foreigners who worshiped a strange God. It would be 400 years before God's people would be able to escape and settle in the land of Canaan. Yet it did not end there, as several times the Israelites were held in captivity by other nations.

Israel clearly understood what it meant to be foreigners in a strange land. And God regularly called them to be kind and hospitable to the foreigner: "Do not oppress an alien; you yourselves know how it feels to be aliens, because you were aliens in Egypt"

(Exod. 23:9). The New Testament carries this theme forward. Jesus told His followers that they would always be foreigners in this world (see John 15:19). And the apostle Peter echoed this statement: "Dear friends, I urge you, as aliens and strangers in the world . . ." (1 Pet. 2:11).

The Kingdom we belong to is not of this world. Yes, we live in this world, but we are not of it. Jesus had to remind His disciples and followers that they could not elevate themselves above the foreigner. In fact, He told them that they must love one another—including the foreigner—as they love themselves (see John 13:34).

That is the crux of Jesus' parable of the Good Samaritan (see Luke 10:25-37). A Jew had been beaten up and left by the wayside, but all the other Jews who saw this fellow in his poor condition passed him by. It was a foreigner who lived out the law of love who had compassion for this man and stopped to care for him. A foreigner had all the reason in the world to ignore this man, for the Jewish people despised all others who were not racially Jewish. We might paraphrase the idea this way: Love the foreigner as you love yourself, and then you will have obeyed all the commands of the Lord.

Jesus pushed the disciples on this point several times. The Samaritan woman whom Jesus met at the well would have been considered a half-breed in her day. Yet Jesus not only touched her with tender concern, but He also made such an impact on her that she turned into an evangelist and brought the whole town to meet Him (see John 4:28-30). Again, the twist: a non-Jew showed people the way to God. Paul later summed up this teaching with the statement, "There is neither Jew nor Greek" (Gal. 3:28). This is our official Christian belief. Unfortunately, our lifestyle does not always reflect this belief.

The world today is desperate for the Christian message. Thousands are being killed and millions are being left destitute.

The world does not know how to love the foreigner. It does not know how to accept others as equals. It does, however, know how to hate. And it does so fiercely.

The Church needs to have a clear message of love and acceptance in this time of fission and fracture. We need to be the ones who model the message that we all have been created with full and equal dignity. No one is to be pushed down for the purpose of elevating another. No one should presume himself or herself to be more noble in race than another.

The Church has often been misguided in this respect. It has lent its support to ethnic oppression, justified systems of slavery and apartheid, and condoned the mistreatment of Native Americans—to name just a few past injustices. We need to be redeemed from that history, for it stands counter to the biblical mandates to love the foreigner and the stranger. We as the Body of Christ clearly cannot say we have loved them as we have loved ourselves.

We in the Church can make a fresh start right now. The Holy Spirit will give us the power if we just take that step of faith.

Project 1: Keep the Border Human

Symbols carry immense power to define a nation. Perhaps the one most associated with the United States historically has been the Statue of Liberty. The idea of a nation that opens its arms to the weary, downtrodden and huddled masses is a heady welcome in a world that typically defines its borders with guns, fences and patrols.

Of course, the vision of the Lady has faded over time. At some point in our history, those inside the borders decided, "Enough already. Now it's time to consolidate the wealth of the land around those who already got in." And since the time of the attacks on the

World Trade Center on September 11, 2001, control of the borders has moved from the department of immigration to the newly organized department of homeland security. Fear is a powerful political guide. For a large percentage of Americans, a "secure" border seems to be the only way to guarantee a safe future. Not only has the light on the Lady's torch gone out, but she has also turned her back on those who try to enter her harbor.

As with any other nation in the world, the United States has to determine how many immigrants it will allow legal passage each year, and this number is usually determined by a combination of labor needs and treaties. For example, in 2005, the United States granted 84,681 green cards to immigrants from India that entitled them to become permanent residents in the United States.[1] These individuals' contribution to our economy and the high-end technical services they provide is considered invaluable.[2] Mixing this kind of liberal immigration policy with national unemployment statistics is not always a smooth drink to swallow, but it's an idea that makes enough sense to both Republicans and Democrats that it sticks.

Where the issue becomes particularly contentious and clouded is around our neighbors south of the border—Mexican immigrants. It is estimated that as of 2004, there were approximately 5.3 million undocumented (illegal) Mexican immigrants living in the United States.[3] For many businesses, the presence of these illegal immigrants is a plus, because they work hard, they work long hours, they are willing to be paid a wage below the minimum wage (under the table), and they take no benefits. Agricultural farms, in particular, rely heavily on an influx of undocumented staff during the harvest season.

On the one hand, the government tolerates this reality because there seems to be large economic benefits to the country. And yet, there is the feeling among a number of U.S. citizens that these immigrants are stealing jobs, flooding the hospitals and schools for services that are subsidized by legal tax payers, or bringing in crime, drugs and prostitution. Volunteer posses have emerged in some regions of the border states to police these zones.

To much of the nation's surprise, during April 2006, hundreds of thousands of Americans took to the streets to support a more generous public policy toward illegal immigrants from Mexico. More than 100,000 people rallied in Phoenix, Arizona, in support of the immigrants.[4] It was the largest rally ever held in the history of Phoenix—a city that takes special pride in its conservatism.

The public always debates ideas and policies for the national good, and immigration is no exception. But for some, the process has become a means of dehumanizing refugees. For instance, in the past, concerned citizens have reached out to the refugees as they attempt to cross the desert plains of Arizona, where much of the illegal movement occurs. However, local, state and federal bodies have begun to criminalize any assistance offered to these illegal immigrants as they cross the desert plains in search of a better life.

The religious community in southern Arizona recently decided to place itself against the law on this issue. The position they have taken is that all God's children deserve a cup of water in the desert, regardless of their life circumstance. According to these individuals, to make it a criminal act to provide sustenance in a life-threatening situation is to go against God's laws, and so these activists started an organization called Humane Borders. Humane Borders has since established more than 70 watering stations throughout the desert. Each station is marked with flags on 30-foot poles, and the large blue water drums (donated by local businesses) are clearly marked with the word *agua*. Thousands of volunteers assist in keeping the water supplied, looking out for at-risk refugees, and documenting how these individuals are being treated by the legal system.

We all need to be reminded that people who are in search of a living are *human beings*. It's repulsive to criminalize the act of providing a cup of water to a person in need. We encourage volunteers in Arizona to link up with Humane Borders to keep the borders human. To join their effort, or to gain ideas from them to use in your own region, go to the organization's website at www.humane borders.org.

Another border organization, BorderLinks, sponsors one- to five-day binational education trips to the Mexican-U.S. border. The idea is to keep the conversation going about what it means to be neighbors and to retain the sense of each other's identity. The educational trips include several meetings with local people and discussion on issues such as immigration policy, human rights and culture. BorderLinks also offers a semester-long academic program.

Anything to advance our understanding of shared humanity gets the thumbs up from us! You can contact BorderLinks at www.borderlinks.org.

Project 2: Host a Refugee Family

The U.S. Committee for Refugees estimates that there are more than 15 million refugees in the world today.[5] These are people who, for a number of reasons, have been forced to leave their homes in search of safety.

Often, we tend to think of refugees in terms of people who are victims of weather-related events or earthquakes (floods, droughts, hurricanes, tsunamis). But the greatest numbers of refugees in the world today have been displaced as a consequence of war—be it civil war or cross-border wars. These people's lives have been shattered by bombs dropping from the sky, marauders on the ground, forced relocations and raw fear.

Approximately 80 percent of the deaths that occur in war are civilian deaths. Although the international community has agreed to a host of rules as to how nations are to engage in war, those rules are rarely observed during battle. Whereas civilians used to be considered off-limits to the designs of war, they are now central to war strategy. Entire cities are forced to evacuate, villages are terrorized with bombings, crops are burned, and water, power and sewer systems are destroyed—endangering the thousands of families who depend upon them. In the twentieth century alone, more than 100 million civilians died as a result of war.[6]

Refugees who flee their countries of origin to escape atrocities in their homelands often wind up virtually imprisoned by the new circumstances they encounter once they cross the border. Many countries have no control over their refugee influx and place the refugees in camps with inadequate security, health care and sanitation. To make matters worse, the refugees may often end up as pawns in negotiations between warring countries.

Refugees hope that their status is temporary. Human beings in general love their homeland, wish to be reunited with it, and hold on to the idea that the conflict will resolve and peace will return. But that is not always the case. Some refugee communities relocate permanently to other nations, where they have to take on a new language, culture and social identity. The transitions are confusing, emotionally taxing, economically stressful, and often filled with experiences of prejudice.

One of the organizations most focused on refugee relocation in the United States is Catholic Relief Services. This organization's mission is to help refugee families through the transition of arriving in this foreign country and establishing themselves in a community. There are many tasks involved in that transition:

finding a job; enrolling children in a local school; learning the medical, legal and banking systems; finding a home; and learning the language—just to name a few.

Catholic Relief Services seeks individuals or groups who are willing to host a family during the entire transition process, and provides all the assistance volunteers need to perform this type of work. This project is especially ideal for individuals who want to be a practical partner in people's lives and gain a new understanding of the customs, beauty and heartaches that have been transported halfway across the globe.

If you or someone you know is interested in hosting a family, or if you want more information on how this process works, visit the Catholic Relief Service's website at www.crs.org.

Project 3: Make Friends with International Students

People from around the world find the United States a good place to receive their undergraduate and/or postgraduate education. Our campuses serve as a meeting place of nations. Because of this, there are tremendous opportunities for Christians to build bridges with people from these other cultures.

Here are a few suggestions as to how you, your friends or those in your church can develop friendships with international students:

- **Join an Outreach Program.** International Students, Inc. is a nonprofit ministry that helps Christians host international students. If they have a chapter on your local college campus, become involved and ask them to help you catch the vision (www.isionline.org).

- **Launch an Outreach Program.** If there is no International Students, Inc. chapter in your area, contact the organization and ask them to help you organize one through your church or local college. Take the lead in your area and be a catalyst for launching a quality outreach to foreign students.

- **Provide Student Orientation.** Contact your local college or university and offer to help out with international student orientation. If you simply present yourself as a volunteer to their program, they will likely accept your participation. This will give you the opportunity to provide practical assistance to foreign students as they adjust to this culture, and it will open the door for a deeper relationship with them in the days ahead.

- **Open Your Home.** Consider opening your home as a boarding option for international students. Universities are often looking for these kinds of leads because they have discovered that students adjust much more easily when given this kind of specific attention. Perhaps you know friends or people at church who would also like to open their homes in this way.

Look for ways to connect with international students in your school, church or neighborhood. Attend any cultural events you hear about on campus or in your community. This will give you an appreciation for other cultures and, again, open the door for future relationships.

Project 4: Celebrate Community

We live in a world that has become smaller because of technology. What used to be a month-long ship ride for the few has become a several-hour flight for the many. Millions of instantaneous e-mail and text messages link hundreds of millions of people across thousands of miles. Without a second thought, we purchase and exchange materials online with merchants from another culture, time zone and nation.

Yet for all the connectedness in the globe, we are a shattered human community. Check the headlines on any given day and there is a story about an ethnic minority terrorized by a dominant social group, a church or mosque torched, a gay man murdered, a Jewish immigrant tortured, an indigenous people group forced off the land, a religious tradition ridiculed.

Why it is that we are more willing to destroy others than build bridges with them? At the end of the day, there is no true benefit to diminishing people who are unlike us. Such behavior only makes the world less secure for our children.

Every year, there are several national holidays or observations that celebrate a variety of ethnic and religious traditions. These events display the diversity of the human family and hold the treasured stories, myths and aspirations of people groups from all around the world. One suggestion is to make your campus a place of celebrating the various traditions, ethnicities and stories that are present in our culture.

For example, during particular Jewish, Muslim, Christian or Hindu holidays, you and your fellow students could host a booth in the student center that explains the specific holiday. If the group of students hosting the booth is from diverse religious backgrounds, the event becomes a statement of honor, unity and respect in the midst of diversity. It's a way of saying that people do not have to diminish others in order to celebrate their own tradition. More important, it is a way of welcoming the diversity of the human family and making it safe for human beings to express their faith and their traditions.

During those same holidays, you might also consider writing up stories in the student newspaper that explain the particular day being celebrated. You could offer samplings of foods (if different from the normal fare) at special meetings and events. You could play music and display dress and art forms associated with that holiday for public education.

Some of us fear the loss of our own faith or ethnic traditions when we acknowledge and celebrate the existence of others' traditions. But that way of thinking is counterintuitive. When we isolate ourselves, we create risk and division. Community is not the loss of differences; rather, it is the very place that allows for the coexistence and celebration of those differences.

Organizations

BorderLinks
620 South Sixth Avenue
Tucson, AZ 85701
Phone: 520-628-8263
Fax: 520-740-0242
E-mail: caryn@borderlinks.org
Website: www.borderlinks.org

Catholic Relief Services
P.O. Box 17090
Baltimore, MD 21203
Phone: 410-625-2220
Website: www.crs.org

**Centers for Disease Control
and Prevention**
1600 Clifton Road
Atlanta, GA 30333
Phone: 404-639-3534
Toll-Free: 800-311-3435
Website: www.cdc.gov

Humane Borders
First Christian Church
740 East Speedway Blvd.
Tucson, AZ 85719
Phone: 520-628-7753
E-mail:
humaneborders@gainusa.com
Website: www.humaneborders.org

International Students, Inc.
P.O. Box C
Colorado Springs, CO 80901
Toll-Free: 800-ISI-Team
Website: www.isionline.org

Migration Policy Institute
1400 16th Street NW, Suite 300
Washington, DC 20036
Phone: 202-266-1940
Fax: 202-266-1900
Website:
www.migrationinformation.org

**U.S. Citizenship
and Immigration Services**
20 Massachusetts Avenue NW
Washington, DC 20529
Toll-Free: 800-375-5283
Website: www.uscis.gov

**U.S. Committee for Refugees
and Immigrants**
1717 Massachusetts Avenue NW,
Suite 200
Washington, DC 20036
Phone: 202-347-3507
Fax: 202-347-3418
Website: www.refugees.org

The World

CARING FOR THE PEOPLE OF ALL NATIONS

God is always pursuing the world with His love. This is not just a doctrinal concept—it is personal. Since the beginning of time, God has desired relationship with the crown of His creation. The story of Adam and Eve shows us a God who walked through the Garden for a personal chat with His loved ones (see Gen. 2-3). The story of Abraham reveals a God who desired to make a personal covenant with His creation (see Gen. 15). The story of Moses tells of a God who cared about the suffering of His people and acted on their behalf to free them from oppression under Pharaoh (see Exod. 6-12). The Old Testament is filled with stories of a King who pleads with His followers to remain linked to Him.

Of course, God never intended to give His love *only* to the people of Israel. Rather, through them He intended to bring all of humankind into relationship with Him. When Abraham began his first journey of faith to a place that God would yet show him, Yahweh announced, "I will make your name great, and you will be a blessing . . . and all peoples on earth will be blessed through you" (Gen. 12:2-3). This theme of "all peoples" is a golden thread that winds itself through the Law, the psalms and the prophets.

The Israelites understood that their Lord wanted to raise every valley and lower every mountain to make straight the path that led to the mountain of Zion. The very Temple was designed with a courtyard that was meant to hold the scores of foreigners who would come to worship Yahweh.

Unfortunately, Israel was selfish in its call to spread the good news of Yahweh. Indeed, even the very area in the Temple intended for all nations to worship had been turned into a money-making plaza. When Christ was headed toward the crucifixion, He saw this and cleared the Temple with the judgment, "Is it not written: 'My house will be called a house of prayer for all nations'? But you have made it a 'den of robbers'" (Mark 11:17).

Jesus continued resolutely toward the cross, and as He gave up His last breath, the curtain that barred the public from the Holy of Holies was ripped in two—from top to bottom. The message that God seemed to be communicating through this act was that never again would a people prevent others from enjoying His salvation. The disciples caught on to the notion. Historians tell us that 11 of them died as martyrs on the mission field—Thomas as far away as North India.

The book of Revelation promises us a good ending to the effort of Calvary. One day, members from every tribe, tongue and nation will celebrate the complete and final work of the cross (see Rev. 7:9-10).

God wills that none should perish. We, His Church, have the same heart to see sinners saved. And we are called to establish His love in all the earth.

Project 1: Without Borders

In 1832, a young Swiss businessman named Henri Durant wrote of the carnage he had witnessed on a battlefield in Italy and proposed forming a neutral organization devoted to caring for the sick and wounded of war. His efforts led to the formation of the International Committee of the Red Cross in 1863 and the formation of an international convention shortly thereafter in Geneva, Switzerland.[1] For Durant, it was clear that there needed to be a way to tend the afflicted without reference to their political orientation. Indeed, the Geneva Conventions were first penned to protect enemy soldiers in combat—the temptation of the victors to abuse their captives was just too great.

Today, a number of new nongovernmental organizations "without borders" are emerging around the globe. Although some people on the political continuum fear these types of organizations as being a kind of One World Order, these without-borders-style organizations are in fact the opposite of being world-order-oriented. Their ethic of human service to all frees them from bowing to the interests of government or industry. The beauty of their efforts is that they deliver services to every part of the world in which human suffering exists amid conflicts of loyalty.

There are three particular without-borders organizations that we would like to highlight for you to check into—and hopefully get involved with. The first organization, Doctors Without Borders, was the pioneer of this phenomenon. Doctors Without Borders originated in France during the Cold War, when the world was divided between conflicting capitalistic and communistic political ideologies. In times of war or crises, civilians often could not get food, aid or medical care because they were identified by other nations as having the "wrong" political persuasion. Doctors Without Borders was able to enter those zones and provide critical care to those in need.

Over time, Doctors Without Borders has also been able to provide accurate medical assessments of situations that would normally be considered political in a time of war. For example, an outbreak of cholera or an AIDS epidemic could be considered a propaganda tool in a war zone. Information on epidemics is often viewed with suspicion, and responses from the medical community can be affected as a result. Doctors Without Borders has a solid reputation for serving no political interest—only those who suffer. To connect with them, visit their website at www.doctorswithout borders.org.

The military has never loved the press, and yet the press is one of the only tools available to the public to keep the military honest. Reporters Without Borders, the second organization that we would like to highlight, has emerged to be a teller of truth in times of war and in countries in which political oppression exists. Unlike the "embedded" reporters who travel to war zones under the protection of military units, these reporters do not seek the protection of the military in any context, nor do they agree to any limits on what they are willing to report back to the public. They oppose the elitist view of governments worldwide that claim the public does not know how to evaluate or understand the truth of their nation's actions during conflicts.

Reporters Without Borders has a very helpful website on how to become involved as an amateur blog reporter. The organization's site is also a great place for a college student to begin an honest career in human rights reporting. You can contact Reporters Without Borders at www.rsf.org.

The third organization, Engineers Without Borders, comprises engineers from around the world who look for ways to partner with people groups across borders to find truly sustainable ways of applying technology for the benefit of all human beings. The organization believes that no one should try to impose a technological "fix" on another culture and that the best way for engineers to enter a society is under the auspices of an existing local group that will ultimately own the outcome of the engineering project. The engineers that comprise this organization are neutral to community ideology and, as with the other without-borders organizations, seek to bring health and a bright future to all people of the world without respect to their political affiliations.

Engineers Without Borders is a great organization for engineering students to check out, especially if they are looking for ways to expand their horizons and serve humanity over their summer break. You can contact them at www.ewb-usa.org or www.ewb-international.org.

Project 2: Buy Nothing Day

What is it about sliding that credit card through a reader? Psychologists think that people actually derive the same sensation by using their credit card as they do eating food. That sound of the card swiping can produce the same gratifying feeling as does a bit of good food going down the gullet. Strange, indeed, but sadly very true!

In an almost disturbing coincidence, in the United States the day of the year with the highest foot traffic in shopping malls is typically the day after Thanksgiving. In fact, among many retailers, this day has become known as "Black Friday" because it indicates the time when sales figures typically go from red to black. People go from stuffing their bellies with turkey one day to cramming their bags with stuff the next.

Surely, the notion of giving thanks shouldn't lead us to a near orgy of spending. Wouldn't it make sense that after a time of pause every year when we give thanks for having so much, we would also put a pause on our consuming? Sadly, it seems that Thanksgiving shines a spotlight on our insatiable desire to have more, not our heart's gratitude for what we have received. It is especially disturbing that in a world of so much desperate poverty, "thanksgiving" in our society is followed by heartless disregard for those who have nothing.

Buy Nothing Day came about as a response to the madness of this consumerism. This movement, which now has affiliates in more than 20 countries around the world, is not against consuming (if it were, it would have to be pro-death). Rather, it is against the "ism" of consuming—a lifestyle of mindlessly acquiring more because the culture has convinced us of the need to shop. Those who participate in the Buy Nothing Day simply pledge to buy nothing on the day after Thanksgiving. It seems to be a highly appropriate way of taking back this holiday!

Buy Nothing Day can be a time of lovely celebration centered around ways to add value to your life without adding junk to your closets. For example, instead of going to the mall, you could spend the time with friends over a community meal, attend a free concert in the park, or just take a long hike. And, of course, counter to one college student's suggestion, the idea is *not* to make up all that consuming on another day!

If you think about it, the point of a sale at a store is not to add value to your life, but to get you to buy. So when you agree to give in to the post-Thanksgiving sales pitch, you are simply agreeing to add money to the coffers of corporations that have decided it would be best to get you up from the couch and walk the turkey off with your credit card. Why give Thanksgiving weekend to the whims of Madison Avenue when it could instead be a sacred moment of celebration for all the bounty that already defines your life?

To connect to the Buy Nothing Day movement, visit their website at www.buynothingday.org.

Project 3: Water for All

It's always difficult to wrap our minds around numbers that come with nine zeros, but the fact is that one *billion* people in the world today—one out of every six humans—have no access to safe drinking water. And 2.6 billion people, or roughly 40 percent of the global population, do not have basic sanitation services.[2] The problem is so severe that at the World Water Forum held in March 2006, representatives from 140 countries deliberated on the goal of cutting in half by 2015 the proportion of people around the world who do not have sustainable access to safe drinking water.[3]

One measure of poverty used by development organizations is the number of hours each day people spend in search of potable water. For some, that is a daily quest that takes more than two hours. For most of us in the United States, it's half a second—a simple twist of the wrist. We are fortunate that we have no water woes. If only the rest of the world could say the same. Instead, the poorest of the poor ingest water that makes their lives worse.

Water is not a neutral commodity but is highly politicized. Wars are fought over the rights to it, and nations have entered into complex treaties about its appropriate use. At the local level, the issue of who has the rights to the water must also be resolved. Can someone dump waste into a river if others downstream will be affected? Can someone upstream dam a river to ensure enough water year round for his or her crops? Can a person divert a river to his or her central plains to interrupt a drought season that threatens that individual's food production? Does it matter if pesticides from that person's orange grove leach into the aquifer and pollute drinking wells a few miles away?

For decades, companies have been scouring the globe to secure the rights to other people's water. For example, a company in Santiago, Chile, recently bought up water rights to many regions in Iowa. One day, farmers in that state will be sending their monthly water payments to another country. Coca-Cola and Pepsi have also secured the water rights in key regions of several countries throughout the world.

Some have raised the question in ethical terms: Does anyone have the right to control another person's access to water when it is a matter of basic health and survival? It's an important question to wrestle with because it sits at the core of future civilization. Already, massive protests around the world have erupted over access to water. Global bodies, such as the International Monetary Fund and the World Bank, when making development loans to poorer countries have insisted that those countries privatize water delivery and/or charge a basic use fee. Of course, the privatization and the fee do not greatly impact those who have good jobs or who enjoy good wealth. It's the poor who suffer.

But the poor are not without advocates: More and more water-activist movements have emerged to upset the West's view of water as a resource for profit. In fact, some countries have been building access to water into their public code as a basic human right. Each citizen is guaranteed enough water each day to address his or her health and sanitation needs. That policy is as right-headed as guaranteeing every child immunization against diseases.

What can you do? One idea is to organize campaigns on your college campus or in your community that will affect our government's policy on water rights for the poor. Raise awareness of any trade and loan policies the U.S. State Department negotiates with poor countries that would make it more difficult for the poor to have access to safe water. Also, consider that in 2002, the U.S. government agreed to help fund a portion of the global campaign (coordinated through the United Nations) to ensure safe and sustainable access to water. However, the United States has not yet met its financial commitments to that campaign. We urge students and others concerned about the plight of the poor in the world to work to bring this issue to light.

To learn more about the World Water Forum initiatives, go to www.worldwaterforum.org. To join the global effort to bring safe water to all, contact the World Water Council at www.world watercouncil.org.

Project 4: Journey for Peace

The typical reflex action to an offense is to hit back: an eye for an eye, a life for a life. In the end, what is achieved is more blindness and death. Not a very good outcome!

As strange as it sounds, a hairdresser has to go through more formal training to cut hair than a president of a nation has to go through to lead a country during times of international conflict. It should not be a mystery that conflict escalates so often to violence in many nations when you consider that most conflict skills of men (which is what most world leaders are) were learned in the sand box. We graduate from college with the training to make money and build empires, but almost never are we required to graduate with a certificate on how to build peace.

The world is desperately in need of models for how to seek and build peace. How do nations step aside from the natural inclination to hit back? How do leaders look strong without having to stand in front of tanks or land their planes on aircraft carriers? How do communities transition from a time of gross human rights violations toward a future of peace without seeking vengeance?

One of the world's most famous political prisoners, Nelson Mandela, led the country of South Africa from a period of apartheid in which 35 million blacks were forced to live as slaves and into a new era of democracy that sought a way to forgive human rights violators rather than punish them. Mandela partnered with Archbishop Desmond Tutu to create the now famous Truth and Reconciliation Commission. For four years, this Commission offered perpetrators of the Apartheid era a forum for publicly confessing their crimes against human beings. The reward for full and truthful disclosure was political amnesty.[4]

Imagine, forgiveness as a political act for confessing your sins against the nation! More than 7,000 political operators came forward to confess their crimes against humanity in the full glare of television cameras.[5] And, to date, not a single confession has led to an act of retribution. That nation truly chose to seek peace instead of vengeance.

There's a lot to learn from South Africa's story. Perhaps one of the most scandalous elements of the apartheid years was that those who originally constructed and led that system of oppression were Christians. In 1948, the National Party, under the leadership of protestant cleric Daniel Francois Malan, came into power in South Africa and implemented the Group Areas Act of 1950, which effectively set the foundation of the apartheid system.[6]

The predominately white Dutch Reformed Church supported the action, arguing that God is the "Great Divider" (in Genesis 1, He separated everything into categories—light from dark); that whites should have more opportunities because they heed God's "favor"; that races should remain "pure"; and that people are only spiritually equal, but not physically equal.[7] They used their sacred texts to validate their crimes against humanity, claiming they were honoring the diversity of God's family while also protecting the nation.

If you are seeking a future in community development, international politics or peace-building, an excellent six- to eight-week intensive course on peace-building is held each summer in the

Republic of South Africa. Based out of the city of Cape Town at the very southern tip of Africa, this program allows students to meet with community, political, religious and volunteer leaders to learn about how the nation chose peace over violence. Students are placed in internships with indigenous organizations to learn how to build a society on the other side of violence. Courses include Human Rights, Transitional Justice, and Religion as a Source of Peace and Violence. Outside of class time, students live in the homes of South Africans who were oppressed. (It's possible to take the intensive summer course for credit or to simply audit it.)

Studying for peace is really about taking a journey. Students who travel to South Africa to learn from that nation's process of overcoming violence soon discover that the way of peace raises demanding questions about their own intellect, heart, nation and view of patriotism. They find that the road to building peace is a constant journey that requires shedding those parts of their lives that prevent them from embracing the humanity of others—that prevent them from honoring the stories, faith and aspirations of peoples, nations and groups that are very different from their own.

To read more about the Truth and Reconciliation Commission in South Africa, visit the South African Government's website at www.info.gov.za or the Truth and Reconciliation home page at www.doj.gov.za. For information on how to enroll in the program on peace-building, contact the South Africa Community Fund through their website at www.southafricacommu nityfund.org.

Project 5: Encourage Working Abroad

The old term for it was "tentmaking." Simply put, it is the idea that your missionary work is funded by your job.

Today, hundreds of thousands of North American Christians live abroad and are employed by secular companies. Their responsibilities include activities as diverse as teaching, administrating hospitals, promoting government programs, designing sewer systems, and managing telecommunications systems. These people enjoy the benefits of a regular salary, medical coverage, vacation and extended-leave options back home—often paid for by their employer.

This is welcome news for those who are gifted at serving God overseas but not skilled at fund-raising. A typical missionary family today is expected to raise upward of $60,000 a year, with monthly support ranging between $1,000 to $8,500 based on cost-of-living factors, number of family members, child education costs, ministry expenses and start-up costs.[8] As a result, hundreds of eager missionary-families-in-waiting give up after a few years of going from church to church in search of funds but without raising an adequate amount.

The tentmaking option is not a cop-out for people who could not—or did not want to—raise support. It is a marvelous gift from God that makes the likelihood of missionary service real for thousands of people. However, taking advantage of these contemporary opportunities will require each of us to adjust our traditional views on evangelism and missions work.

If you are interested in the tentmaking option, talk to your friends and family and those whom you trust about the idea of taking a job abroad. Share your vision of ministering overseas while working for a company that will foot the bill. If you are excited about it, perhaps you could even challenge your friends and loved ones to consider doing it with you and going on a one- or two-year work option to another culture. If some show interest, pray together regularly and begin to plot a course of action.

You can also get help from tentmaking organizations such as Intent (formerly the United States Association of Tentmakers) at www.intent.org; the Business Professionals Network at www.bpn.org; and Christian Resource Ministries at www.crmlead ers.org. These groups will help minimize your frustrations and maximize your ministry opportunities. Some keep an up-to-date listing of international job openings. And don't forget to enlist financial and prayer support from your church. Ask for friends and family to commit to praying for you regularly and, if possible, ask them to visit you while you're abroad.

Project 6: Travel Abroad

Perhaps the best way to continually broaden your understanding of the world, provided you have the means, is to simply travel abroad. When you regularly brush against the pain and poverty of the different cultures of the world, it will become difficult for you to intellectualize the experience or just shrug it off. The need in the world becomes real and tangible and keeps your commitment to reaching others sharp and alive. You are forced to ask, "Lord, what will You have me do?"

Wherever you go and however you get there, we recommend the following guidelines when planning your annual trip:

- **Go for Variety.** If you were in Brazil last year, go to Japan this year and then Kenya next year. If you visited the slums last year, stay in a high-rise this year and a rural area next year. Try to expose yourself to various forms of government and even dominant religions.

- **Take a Lesson.** Take a language class on occasion to get you closer to the country you intend to visit. Several two-week options are available that will help you gain intensive exposure to Spanish, French and German, to name a few. Language is a key that lets you into different cultures.

- **Visit Theological Institutions.** It is not often that we have the opportunity to see how closely our theological views reflect the fabric of our culture. The broad array of Third World and European seminaries can make for an invaluable lesson in culture. Exposure to another culture's theological tenets can open up concepts or portions of Scripture that earlier were a mystery or seemingly irrelevant.

If you are a student, remember that many colleges and universities offer study-abroad options. The experience of taking a class overseas for a semester will give you a broader perspective on real-world issues and will most likely be something that you will remember for the rest of your life.

Organizations

Buy Nothing Day
E-mail: xymyl@nothing.net
Website: www.buynothingday.org

Christian Resource Ministries
1240 N. Lakeview Ave., Suite 120
Anaheim, CA 92807
Toll-Free: 800-777-6658
Phone: 714-779-0370
Fax: 714-779-0189
E-mail: crm@crmleaders.org
Website: www.crmleaders.org

Doctors Without Borders
333 7th Avenue, 2nd Floor
New York, NY 10001
Phone: 212-679-6800
Fax: 212-679-7016
Website:
www.doctorswithoutborders.org

Engineers Without Borders
1880 Industrial Circle, Suite B3
Longmont, CO 80501
Phone: 303-772-2723
Fax: 303-772-2699
Website: www.ewb-usa.org or
www.ewb-international.org

Intent
615 California Ave.
South Bend, IN 46616
Website: www.intent.org

**International Committee
of the Red Cross**
1100 Connecticut Avenue NW,
Suite 500
Washington, DC 20036
Phone: 202-587-4600
Fax: 202-587-4696
E-mail: washington.was@icrc.org
Website: www.icrc.org

Reporters Without Borders
5 Rue Geoffroy-Marie
75009 Paris, France
Phone: (33) 1-44-83-8484
Fax: (33) 1-45-23-1151
E-mail: rsf@rsf.org
Website: www.rsf.org

South Africa Community Fund
P.O. Box 10777
Tempe, AZ 85284
E-mail: southafricafund@aol.com
Website:
www.southafricacommunityfund.org

Truth and Reconciliation
Private Bag X81
Pretoria 0001
South Africa
Phone: (012) 315-1111
Fax: (012) 357-1112
Internet: www.doj.gov.za

World Water Council
Espace Gaymard
2-4 Place d'Arvieux
13002 Marseille, France
Phone: (33) 4-91-99-4100
Fax: (33) 4-91-99-4101
Website: www.worldwatercouncil.org

World Water Forum
Insurgentes Sur #2416
4th Fl. South Wing
México, D.F. Del. Coyoacán
Col. Copilco el Bajo CP 04340
E-mail: feedback@worldwater
forum4.org.mx
Website: www.worldwaterforum.org

Take Action

IDEAS FOR HEALTHY ACTIVISM

As we come to the last section of the book, we hope that you have found this collection of ideas and resources to be helpful as you seek to serve your community and the world. We believe that the Body of Christ, the Church, is God's special agent of love and that the community of faith is the place in which the very idea of forgiveness, charity and hope should be lived out. Each of us, bonded together, is the gospel for the world today—the Body of Christ in living action. Could there be anything better for the world?

If we were to sum up the spirit of this book, we would say it is all about *life*. "The thief comes only to steal and kill and destroy," Jesus said. "I have come that they may have life, and have it to the full" (John 10:10). What the Church has to offer to the world is the fullness of life. We are a sanctuary, a place of healing and warmth, a base of courage and vision that compels its members to live in the cauldron of human misery. The people of God give hope to the hopeless, pointing to a day when Christ shall wipe away every last tear. If this does not excite you, you need to experience the Resurrection!

We have a vision of Christians feeding the hungry, clothing the naked, giving water to the thirsty, visiting the sick and imprisoned, and caring for the orphan and the widow. We have a vision of Christians who care for the baby in the womb, the child in the Third World ghetto, the elderly in the convalescent center, and the hurting person inside each of our hearts. We have a vision of the Body of Christ advocating on behalf of the oppressed and dispensing tenderness to the downtrodden. We have a vision of a community of believers in which the ideas of brokenness, forgiveness, honor and dignity are not doctrines, but ways of life.

Have we lost our senses? No, we have found them. And we believe that you have as well. We have all imbibed the wine of Christ's Calvary love and are now alive to the vision of the Kingdom and its unfathomable offer of life to all God's children. We know that the world longs for this kind of Jesus—for this kind of flesh-and-blood body of believers.

How will the world know the Messiah has come? Will they hear it in our carefully crafted doctrinal statements, our ecclesiastical rules, or in our order of service? The prophet Isaiah gives us a clue:

> Is not this the kind of fasting I have chosen: to loose the chains of injustice and untie the cords of the yoke, to set the oppressed free and break every yoke? Is it not to share your food with the hungry and to provide the poor wanderer with shelter—when you see the naked, to clothe him, and not to turn away from your own flesh and blood? *Then your light will break forth like the dawn, and your healing will quickly appear; then your righteousness will go before you, and the glory of the LORD will be your rear guard* (Isa. 58:6-8, emphasis added).

The light of the world is seen through the visible acts of God's representatives, His children. This is the life that we bring to the world. This is the high calling of the Church today.

Project 1: Slam Poetry

Political and social dissent is crucial to the health of any society. When governments, businesses or religious groups discourage the free exchange of ideas, we have to wonder what they are hiding or what they fear. One way to diminish the power of such entities is to disagree with their practices or to question their deeds. Slam poetry is an excellent means for the public to enter into that process.

The structure for slam poetry is in the grand old tradition of the "open mic." Open mic nights allow anyone in a community to come forward to try out his or her songs, poetry or other creative forms of expression in a public setting (in the past, they have even provided the launching point for several new performing artists). Slam poetry, however, is a little more directed than the open-mic format—it provides a platform specifically for those individuals who wish to articulate their social or political dissent. No particular point of view is encouraged, as that would be a form of stifling the public voice. Rather, the public is simply invited to rage against the night, however they might experience it.

Slam poetry nights are effective if hosted regularly (for example, every Thursday night) at the same location in a community. People enter a weekly rhythm. A particular host becomes the familiar face who walks guests through the evening. The most effective slam events have a regular band that accompanies the poetry recitation. The band creates a tune around the words and pace of the performer, adding another layer of creativity to the evening. It's not uncommon for the band to create a congregation-like feeling in which, by the end of the evening, people are co-creating and voicing new statements of dissent, singing along, dancing and generally having a really wonderful time of stating their case in a public sphere. However, what is really happening is that a form of accountability is being brought into the public sphere around issues of social importance. People who might otherwise feel disempowered in a particular social system are now able to move forward without restraint. Many will even find themselves preparing in advance each week to voice their opinions, whatever they happen to be.

It's important to normalize a public process that speaks back to power. At the very least, silence suggests disinterest and, at the worst, collusion. Slam poetry evenings are not only a way that people can make their own thoughts known but also provide the means by which they can speak up on behalf of those who have no voice—those who are too remote to be heard, those who are perhaps languishing in prison unjustly, those who cannot speak "our" language and yet are negatively impacted by various policies, or those who face retribution or severe punishment for speaking their minds. If we do not live as a free society, then we, in fact, are not free.

Project 2: Silent Comment

The "silent comment" form of protest is at the other end of the spectrum. At first, the idea of commenting "silently" may seem absurd or contradictory. However, it is actually an effective way for people to say something powerful about what is wrong in the world—without saying anything at all.

The first time we observed students at a university participate in silent comment was around the issue of torture. Recently, several political leaders have opposed the U.S. government's approach to pursuing forms of torture for Iraqis who are considered enemies of the U.S. government's goals in Iraq. While on the one hand the White House has made the case to Congress as to why the United States needed the freedom to dismiss the Geneva Conventions in the Iraqi invasion, others, such as former Secretary of State Colin Powell, have pushed for the United States to serve as an example in the global arena and oppose all forms of torture. Powell has been supported by Senator John McCain, who spent five years as a prisoner of war in Vietnam.

At the silent comment we observed, students dressed in attire from the Middle East stripped down to their undergarments, put hoods over their heads, and lay on the ground handcuffed in a public setting. No words were said—just a stark, silent form of articulating protest. The students stayed in those positions for an hour and were completely vulnerable to what the public did to them. The idea, in this case, was not to state a particular view on torture but rather to physically raise the picture of people who were vulnerable. In part, the hope was to remind the public of the humanity of the Iraqis and to bring the point so close to home that people could not pretend the issue didn't exist.

The primary mechanism of silent comment is to find a visual image that will make an impression on the public—one that will hopefully impact discussions in classrooms, in articles in student newspapers and in other gatherings such as religious meetings, fraternity events or student clubs.

Project 3: See It, Film It, Change It

If a picture paints a thousand words, the video camera tells the heart of the story. How many moving images do we have in our minds from the past few decades of history? Picture the wracked, starved bodies of Holocaust survivors lining up along a barbed-wire fence; the shuttle Challenger exploding into projectiles in midair; a solitary figure holding a tank at bay in Tiananmen Square; an African-American washed down the street with water cannons and being chased by vicious police dogs. From all these images we gain a lasting impression of the extent of human degradation that exists in our world.

The video camera has become a great friend to people who suffer human rights abuses. What makes the abuse of another more likely is the lack of accountability on the part of those who are doing the abuse. It's normal for a shroud of secrecy to protect those in power—the people who least need protection!

Perhaps the most celebrated recent U.S. case of this phenomenon was the beating of Rodney King by some Los Angeles policemen. No matter how much authorities tried to justify the relentless clubbing of this citizen, the video image would not convince the public of the police officers' innocence. The public fully expected the legal system to punish the police for the abuse of a civilian. When the all-white jury found in favor of their peers, the city of Los Angeles literally burst into flames. A massive campaign to reform the police department ensued as a result of the public's response to that single videotape.

The video camera has even entered the secret world of military prisons. Now, concerns have emerged in the American consciousness around questions of detention methods and torture.

Music pioneer and human rights activist Peter Gabriel heads up a new organization called Witness. The tag line for his organization is "See it, Film it, Change it"! The idea is simple enough: Distribute as many video cameras as possible in order to make the public aware of human rights abuses around the world. Witness provides video training to "Human Rights Defenders" and puts them to work fully equipped. The range of abuse being documented includes crackdowns on public dissent, executions, starvation, torture and the ill treatment of people with intellectual and physical challenges.

One of the central notions that defined the formation and structure of the early system of government in the United States was the balance of power. There was a sense that people who have power are not able to monitor their own use of that power. If left to their own devices, they would demand less accountability from the public while demanding loyalty from the public, implying that people are not good citizens if they don't trust the government to do what's best for their protection.

As the saying goes, "Power corrupts; absolute power corrupts absolutely." Sadly, these days, people don't seem to ascribe to this belief. In fact, a coworker of ours once heard a former Joint Chief tell an Admiral in Washington, D.C., "Power corrupts; absolute power is really nice!"

Witness is one person's attempt to protect the most vulnerable of society while also keeping those with the most power accountable for their deeds. However, the idea can only work if volunteers get in line. Contact witness at www.witness.org.

Project 4: Alternative Spring Break

The worst possible way to spend spring break is working on a term paper. Spring break is meant to be just that—a *break*, not catch-up time. For a high percentage of college students, young people and others, spring break is the chance to haul three months' worth of laundry off to Mom's, wake up to homemade breakfast, and sit still for five days straight. (Of course, there are also the not-so-mythical spring breaks packed with activities that rival the story of the Prodigal Son!)

In recent years, an alternative option that thousands of college students and others have caught on to is to use the week away from school or work to serve others in the community or abroad. Students volunteer on behalf of the local community, travel to a work project that benefits humankind or the environment, or learn about culture through creative field trips. Some universities actually design alternative spring breaks for their students, with rates that are way too reasonable to resist. For example, Arizona State University sponsors trips that take students into ancient cave systems or to the communities of indigenous peoples. The entire cost for the week-long trip, including transportation, lodging and meals, typically comes out to less than $50. You can check out the trips Arizona State University sponsors at www.asu.edu/altspringbreak.

Why not get together with a group of other students and plan your own alternative break? Here are a few examples of what you could do:

- **Help Out an Organization.** Connect with a local organization that serves people directly (such as a soup kitchen, rescue mission or job training program). Offer to provide some much-needed relief to the staff by doing whatever menial tasks you and your friends could take on in a week. For example, you could clean bathrooms, wash floors, clean windows, do dishes, wash laundry, or take care of the gardening.

- **Go on a Blitz Build.** Join up with Habitat for Humanity's home-builders blitz. The organization always has spring-break builds that it sponsors throughout the United States. Check it out at the Habitat for Humanity website at www.habitat.org/buildersblitz.

- **Go to the Park.** Volunteer with the Parks Service to do some trail maintenance or campground cleanups. As we mentioned previously, preserving the environment is important not only because the earth is our home, but also because it is the home of those who will come after us in the future.

- **Take a Tour with Kids.** Ask your local middle schools and high schools if you can put together a two-day weekend package for kids. Perhaps you could offer a tour of local art and history museums, do a camping trip into a national park, or organize a day of service at the animal rescue center.

- **Pick Up Some Trash.** Offer to help your local city government finally clean up that stretch of road that is always littered with trash or the stream that some hikers seem to abuse with their garbage.

When planning these events, come up with a five-day option so that you will still have some time for personal breathing room and to rest before classes start up again. Make sure the cost is super low and try to convince your university or college to provide the vehicle and gas for the alternative break. Bottom line about an alternative spring break: It adds value to the community or to your personal life. Even just a one-day commitment will give meaning back to the world and to your academic routines.

Project 5: Add Music to the Sidewalks

What can be more stifling about modern life than communities reduced to cement sidewalks, steel buildings, and straight blacktop roads with the occasional landscaping tree? One sociologist has suggested that the loneliest place in the world to be is in a city packed with people. That's mostly because the very structure of a city breeds alienation from nature, from each other, and from beauty.

Here's an idea that could at least bring some beauty back to the sidewalks: Add some live music. Most cities have some kind of provision against "panhandling," a negative term used to describe people who are hurting so badly financially that they are reduced to begging the public for handouts. One form of so-called panhandling is playing an instrument in public in the hope of getting a couple of dimes or a dollar from people passing by. Some towns have banned the public display of music for that reason.

Rather than giving in to the narrow definitions of city council, try a more proactive way of adding music to the sounds of cars, sirens and busses. Ask permission from your local government to do a regular street corner set on certain days of the week and at scheduled times. If you are an aspiring rock artist (which is the dream of 50 percent of teenaged boys), here's your big break. There's probably no better way to test your personal musical abilities or—if you can pull off an acoustic band gig with your friends—to test your group's ability to work together in public performance.

If you'd like to add music to the sidewalks but don't have the skills, just work the system at the university to find out who is hot. The music department will probably tell you who is not, so stay with the informal networks. You will most likely find someone who is willing to give the street performance idea a shot.

Note that we are not suggesting you put on a concert in the park, where at least some beauty remains—we're trying to soften the sidewalks, not the lawn. It would also not be cool, in our opinion, to add music to the mall. Who needs more encouragement to hang out in the belly of consumerism? Rather, add beauty to the drab, monotonous, suffocating grid of streets that require our allegiance to make a living. Become an urban legend for no other reason than for the sake of adding life back to the most mundane setting of our day.

Project 6: Solidarity Sleep Out

When politicians get together to write their laws, it is doubtful that the first question they ask is, "How will this law benefit the poor and disenfranchised?" Most often, the laws that politicians support seem to benefit the people who write them. Well, maybe there is nothing new under the sun: Power corrupts.

Several cities across the United States have progressively codified laws that keep the homeless off the streets or out of their neighborhoods. Imagine: It is illegal in many cities to be homeless! What's next? Outlawing all forms of poverty? Wouldn't that be great if it meant that the lawmakers were responsible for coming up with ways to wipe out poverty? Wiping out homelessness should not be the same as wiping out the homeless. Yet that appears to be how the law often works—to get rid of the people, not the problem.

One East Coast city outlawed homeless people a couple years ago in the dead of winter. Homeless people were sleeping on heating vents as a way to keep from freezing at night. The lawmakers' brilliant idea was to prevent homelessness by not letting the homeless get warm. (Perhaps the idea was that the homeless would catch a bus to sunnier climates and just be homeless in someone else's city?) Once the legislation kicked in, outlawing the homeless, police were authorized to arrest people for ostensibly littering the sidewalks with illegal material—themselves.

A group of conservative Christian college students decided to turn this into an opportunity to change the laws. They silently rounded up large numbers of their friends and colleagues to join the homeless on the sidewalks at night. As the police did their sweeps, they were suddenly confronted with large numbers of shaven, showered, well-dressed people sleeping on the sidewalks. The students were smart enough to secure media coverage of these bright young university folk being arrested for spending the night on the sidewalk. Of course, it had never been the city's intention to arrest large numbers of people who seemed to look like the sort of citizens we want hanging around on our sidewalks! The coldhearted policy was exposed for what it was, and the city had to retreat from its attack on the homeless.

We think this is a perfect way to side with the right side of the law. If your city has a policy that harms the homeless, find a way to join in solidarity and bring the pressure of regular, warmhearted citizens to bear on city hall's shameful policies toward the poor. Send the message to those in public office that sweeping the sidewalks clean of human beings is not an acceptable way to solve the problem of homelessness.

Project 7: Get in the Way of War

Here is a great question posed by the Christian Peacemaker Teams organization: What would happen if Christians devoted the same discipline and self-sacrifice to nonviolent peacemaking that armies devote to war?[1] Since there are more than a billion Christians in the world today, that is not a shabby question![2]

Last year, the top 10 military nations in the world (including the United States, China and Russia) spent more than $700 billion on war and the machinery of war.[3] That number is almost inconceivable. Those same nations spent less than $50 billion on the victims of war. War is a patently bad idea. And the corresponding great idea is peace. This seems so obvious, and yet is so unpopular in our current climate of fear and insecurity.

Christian Peacemaker Teams go to places in the world where war is imminent or prevails. Unarmed citizens literally get in the way of war with their feet. They surround hospitals, lie down on military runways, populate military targets and remind the public that all victims of war are people. They humanize "collateral damage." They call people to a moment of reflection before they bow to the destructive logic of war.

It's no more likely that Christian Peacemaker Teams will stop war from happening in the world than Jesus' personal appearance on Earth will convince all the members of the human race to love their enemies. Sometimes, we have to feed the hungry just because there are hungry people—not because our actions will overcome world hunger. And sometimes, we have to work for peace just because there is war. In the middle of that small act of courage and kindness, perhaps someone, some village or some nation will be spared the label of "enemy."

To learn more about how to join up with Christian Peacemaker Teams, visit their website at www.cpt.org.

Project 8: Reclaim the Beauty

We truly do worship the ultimate Artist. Unfortunately, much of our church life and activism seems to reflect a stoic, bland view of our Creator. Our "art" is limited to a cross above the pulpit, a few prefabricated stained-glass windows, or a picture of Jesus. Our sense of color is limited to a mix of white walls and a few red pew cushions.

It is time to reclaim the beauty in our churches. Go to your church leadership and ask for permission to do something creative with your building or space. You might even want to ask if you could create some kind of outdoor reflective space on the church grounds. You might only be allowed to work on the youth room, a meeting room or a small corner of the sanctuary, but you've got to start somewhere! Here are a few suggestions to get you going:

- **Ask for Artists.** Find out if any art students are members of your church. If so, ask them to create a set of paintings or sculptures that you can use in the space you are allowed to beautify. Encourage the students to move beyond traditional categories and create something people would not expect to see in a church foyer (or youth room, depending on the location). Wall hangings or a bright new color can go a long way toward upgrading the look and feel of a building.

- **Look for Landscapers.** Find out if any hobbyist landscapers are part of your church and ask them to help you suggest ways to bring more beauty and pizzazz into your church. A fresh landscaping of the garden (plus the addition of a sculpture) can add a reflective quality to the outer areas of your church.

- **Get the Green Thumbs.** If the climate in your area is conducive, ask the green thumbs in your congregation to create a cut flower garden on the premises. A generous supply of fresh flowers throughout the building can bring in the living art of our Creator each week.

Most art comes from the stuff of life, the balance of being filled with the glory of God and living like the son of a carpenter. Bringing beauty to our churches in these ways requires just a little resolve and a bit of a free spirit.

Project 9: Chalk the Walk

One method of beautifying your city is to perform music on the sidewalks. Here's another way—that would be anonymous—to brighten the drab cement: Create chalk art on the sidewalks!

A group of art students in Philadelphia do a random midnight "raid" on the urban sidewalks in fall when the city is beginning to feel particularly cold, bland and without feeling. The students purchase large amounts of sidewalk chalk and then, in the space of about one hour, blanket an entire city block's sidewalk with creative, colorful art. They always select a part of town where people will be walking from the subway to their offices. It's a great way, really, to bring some smiles and stress-relief to the city.

This idea is well worth emulating. To bring a bit of variety to the art form, choose specific public holidays that offer an opportunity for infusing hope and inspiration into the common space. Christmas, Hanukah, Ramadan and Thanksgiving would be some examples. Take the core of the message from these seasons or days and spread the good news. Look for ways to articulate the high ideals of the holiday. Bright colors, artistic symbols and slogans could make for a positive addition to the nation's sidewalks.

A second way to chalk the walks would be as a means of raising awareness around a particular social need. For example, on Martin Luther King Jr. Day, decorate the city's sidewalks with visions of interethnic peace and cooperation. On Labor Day, offer up a vision of a fair wage for the urban poor. On Earth Day, cover the sidewalks with graphic daisies and messages of caring for the earth.

The key is to always do the artwork when no one is watching and to do it in a way that keeps the public wondering where it is going to pop up next. If done well, in time the phenomenon will be newsworthy and draw attention to important issues. Never be tempted to give up the identity of the artists who are spreading the love for free, and never use the art form as a means to diminish others.

Project 10: Be Completely Pro-Life

We heard it said when Mother Teresa was alive that "When Mother Teresa speaks, everybody listens." What was it about her that made it possible for her to enter a circle of pro-choice people and have a reasonable conversation, explaining her convictions regarding the injustice of abortion? She never suffered the barrage of criticism aimed at most "religious fanatics." Her voice was not drowned out by the antagonistic accusations that she was anti-women's rights or old-fashioned. Why was this the case?

Integrity has its own power. Long before Mother Teresa ever opened her mouth, she lived her life. The world came to conclude that she was a saint because of her lifestyle and because of her obvious sacrificial spirit and love for those who were oppressed. When she spoke of her love for the child in the womb, she backed it up by loving those that society abandoned on the other side of the womb.

That is what it means to be completely pro-life—caring for the vulnerable unborn *and* the vulnerable who have been born. The world will never be able to hear the morals or values that drive our pro-life message until we live moral lives. We must be the people who give to the poor, feed the hungry, and give shelter to the homeless. We must be a community of faith that feels no disjunction in teaching English to immigrants, holding hands with friends who have AIDS, pushing for fair housing regulations, opposing racist practices in local business and advocating for unborn rights. We *should* feel the disjunction of proclaiming our love for the life that we cannot see while ignoring the life that we can see. The Scriptures have something to say about that!

No, we must be the ones who champion *all* of life. Always ask yourself the question, "Is my pro-life stance a reality in the way I touch all of life, or is it merely a slogan?" The answer to that question could lead to all sorts of new activity.

Project 11: Raging Grannies

Who would imagine grandmas lining up for military service and being arrested for it? Well, it actually happens!

An international movement that sprang up in Canada in 1987 has become a growing geriatric group to contend with. With now more than 50 chapters spread throughout a dozen countries, the Raging Grannies use the weapons of satire, song and their outrageous personalities to contend against issues such as consumerism and militarism. They've been spotted at shopping malls at Christmas, encouraging shoppers to cut up their credit cards and spread love instead of debt around the season of giving. In California, the group was allegedly spied on by a unit of the National Guard after organizing a Mother's Day anti-war rally.[4] In Arizona and New York, members of the group were arrested for suggesting that the military bring the boys back from the war in Iraq and let them go in their place, seeing as they were already old and ready to die.[5]

These older women are pretty proud of their retirement! Check out what the group has said about its members on its website:

Wearing outlandish hats and warbling witty lyrics, they poke fun at the powerful people who are wreaking havoc with their grandchildren's world. But in spite of their lighthearted approach, their purpose is extremely serious. The Grannies have challenged nuclear-armed ships, forestry companies, arms manufacturers, multinational corporations, pharmaceutical giants, manufacturers of war toys, the World Trade Organization, and every level of government, from municipal councils to the American presidency.[6]

If you find this group interesting, you might want to go to the Raging Grannies website to see if there is a group near your community (note that the events the group sponsors tend to be highly political and controversial). If there is, contact them and see if they would let you sponsor a campus event centered around an issue of social importance at your local college or in a nearby public space. If there's not a group near you, maybe it's time to talk to your grandma—and get her motivated! You can get into the Internet world of Raging Grannies at www.raging grannies.com.

Project 12: Earth Food

Understanding the label on a food package requires a degree in pharmacology. The good old days of community markets that sold normal-looking vegetables and fruits from local farms have been replaced with truly strange food that is all shined up and perfectly shaped (like we are supposed to be doing with our bodies as well!). If we want to buy fresh produce that is not laced with toxic inputs and lab-produced growth chemicals, then we have to pay a higher price. Old-fashioned food produced by the earth's normal rhythms is out. Modern eating offers up an amazing array of carcinogens and substances whose long-term effects on our bodies is yet unknown.

It's not as though modern food has made us healthy. Doctors report an alarming increase in childhood obesity, and the adult physical calamities related to food abound. So much for the triumph of advanced technology around our dinner tables!

Given what we know about the dangers of modern food production, our culture has a funny way of marginalizing people who choose to be careful about the food they buy and eat. In some ways, we are a schizophrenic society. For decades now, our society has supported national campaigns that bar cigarette companies from advertising their products on television and has required those companies to trumpet the dangers related to their product. This seems to fit in a culture that tells kids to be careful when crossing the street and that fines drivers who don't wear seat belts. But our culture is not so kind to people who choose to eat carefully. We deride consumers who eat "weeds and seeds," and stereotypes persist around humans who want to limit the amount of chemically infused food they put into their blood stream.

We might need to ask, "Why are we so afraid of healthy eating?" And perhaps the next question is, "Why do we trust giant food manufacturers?" Food companies' primary mission is to make money, not to produce health. If you question that premise, ponder why it is that the major tobacco firms own a large share of our food-producing corporations in the nation today. As long as we reward these corporations with our dollars, they will continue to serve us up dinner in a toxic cocktail. And even with the clear understanding of the negative impacts of soft drinks on kids, public school systems across the land have happily made room for vending machines throughout their schools. Recently, it took a former U.S. president to convince schools to make their food safe and healthy. How successful these efforts will be in the long run is still to be seen, but at least it is a step in the right direction.

In many ways, eating is a default exercise—without much thought, we just do what we have always done. One suggestion to address this problem is to be mindful of our eating patterns, proactively interrupt what's "normal," and nurture a different view of what role food can take in our lives. Here is a sampling of ideas to try out:

- **Drop the Junk.** Try not to eat any junk food for an entire week. That includes all the chips, soda, fast-food creations (stuffed with grease, salt and who knows what else) and snacks that come in airtight packaging. During that same week, create snacks that are kind to your body—organically grown fruits, nuts and other finger foods.

- **Skip the Snacks.** Just say no to recreational eating. Probably none of us can remember back to the days when eating happened more or less three times a day! Not that we have to go back to the old days, but there is something to say about consuming food to fill our bellies rather than to fill our time. Try it out—don't eat anything between meals: no drinks, no candy, no snacks.

- **Eat Closer to the Earth.** When doing the grocery shopping, look for products that are more organic and less of a laboratory construct. Also, watch the waste— sometimes, we go home with more packaging around our foods than the foods themselves. With all the shrink-wrapping, cans, boxes and bottles, we may well wonder if food was the byproduct of our shopping rather than the main point. It takes effort to shop more carefully and, unfortunately, it costs more to shop healthfully. Yet we need to take the opportunity that has been offered to us as consumers to vote with our purchasing patterns and influence the future.

- **Eat with a Sense of the Sacred.** For many in the world, food is about survival. Billions of people live way too close to the edge for us to be flagrant about nutrition. Every piece of bread, ear of corn and cup of water is life for a mom, a future for a child. As wealthy people, when we handle food, in some ways we are holding in our palms the very survival of others. We've all heard the joke about the mom who instructs her kids to finish dinner because of the starving masses in some other country. The kid retorts, "What, do you want me to mail it to them?" It's cute on the surface, but it is vile at its core. Hunger and starvation don't happen apart from calamity and greed. When we lose our sense of what it means to live in a world in which people would say a prayer of thanks for a crust of bread, we have lost our sacred center.

- **Eat with a Sense of Delight.** Some could read the paragraph above to be about guilt. It's not—it is about the profound dimension of the sacred. There is a light-hearted dimension to eating as well—delight. One way to move toward a nation of healthy eaters is to discover the genuine delight of food: the smells, the flavors, the varieties, the cultures, the nuance. What happened to those days of sitting around the table bragging up mom's unbelievable secret pasta recipe, dad's ancient sauce passed down through Great-grandpa, and the kids' first attempts at honest, homemade cookies?

It's not easy to eat healthily in our modern society, but it is worth the effort. We need to take care of our bodies. If we are not motivated to take care of our own bodies, perhaps we will be willing to look out for the bodies of our kids and the earth that produces our nutrition.

Project 13: Give Blood

We have a mystical relationship to blood. Literature of old tries to explain the elements of this liquid and how it gives us life, feeds our personalities and accounts for our spiritual selves. Some of this reading is fascinating, some of it truly bizarre. All of it, however, lifts the lid on the ongoing human need to connect with the source of life.

In the Church, we go much deeper into that mystery. We *do* believe that blood gives us life. We celebrate the blood of Jesus. Through it we have received the forgiveness of sins. Through it we have the gift of eternal life in heaven, where we will enjoy all the benefits of life in its most extravagant and pleasurable forms forever and ever. "No eye has seen, no ear has heard, no mind has conceived what God has prepared for those who love him" (1 Cor. 2:9). All this will happen because of the blood of Jesus.

Here's a suggestion: Organize an annual blood-bank drive at your church by partnering with a local blood bank. Suggest this partnership idea to your church leadership, and then help them make it happen by doing the legwork! Most local blood banks would be more than happy to help you set up a blood drive and provide your church with the resources you need to pull off this project. Some people in the congregation won't be able to give blood or may be unwilling to do so, but the majority will most likely gladly volunteer.

The physical act of giving your blood is a statement of unity with the cross of Christ and equality with the human race. It is a deed that makes us vulnerable to pain, because we care about others' pain. It is a form of giving that literally comes from within. Being pro-life does not get much more poetic than this.

Project 14: Celebrate!

The idea of tithing in the Old Testament does not exactly fit our contemporary bang-'em-on-the-head-to-get-more-bucks model. Back then, tithing was not linked to a building program, utilities or payroll. It was a system that subsidized a party—a great festival honoring Yahweh's goodness, grace and forgiveness. It was a celebration that He remembered the people's sins no more and dealt with the people mercifully.

The Israelites would make their sojourn to the Temple and spend days camping out with family and friends, feasting, drinking, dancing, singing and laughing. Smoke rose to the heavens as the firstfruits were sacrificed in thanksgiving to the Lord. The pyre of death was the altar of life, and all of it went to the Lord. (Caring for the physical needs of others came from the coffers *beyond* the 10 percent.)

Sadly, Christians have lost the party spirit. We have lost the celebration of life. We all could learn a few things from the Israelites of old! For example, why not plan an event around the theme of fun? The beginning of the new year—the time when most of us make resolutions that we typically break within the first month—could be a night of enjoyment rather than a somber time of setting goals. You could invite people from your church or school to decide what would be fun and then accommodate the variety of interests. Some people might enjoy a blowout DVD session of watching five movies in a row; others might enjoy stargazing or having dinner on the beach. Consider the ways that you could provide refreshment and fun to your own neighborhood. One group of volunteers whose church is located in a residential community throws an annual block party. One Saturday a year, they block off both ends of the street with barricades and let loose. It is an all-day mix of arts, crafts, games, barbecues and live music provided by musicians from the church and the neighborhood.

Organizations

Arizona State University
Alternative Spring Break
c/o ASU for Arizona:
Building Great Communities
Mail Code 1608
541 East Van Buren Street, Suite B-5
Phoenix, AZ 85004
Phone: 480-727-5060
E-mail: altsb@asu.edu
Website: www.asu.edu/altspringbreak

**Christian Community
Development Association**
3555 W. Ogden Avenue
Chicago, IL 60623
Phone: 773-762-0994
Fax: 773-346-0071
E-mail: info@ccda.org
Website: www.ccda.org

Christian Peacemaker Teams
P.O. Box 6508
Chicago, IL 60680
Phone: 773-277-0253
Fax: 773-277-0291
E-mail: peacemakers@cpt.org
Website: www.cpt.org

National Right to Life Committee
512 10th Street NW
Washington, DC 20004
Phone: 202-626-8800
E-mail: nrlc@nrlc.org
Website: www.nrlc.org

Raging Grannies
E-mail: info@RagingGrannies.com
Website: www.raginggrannies.com

Witness
80 Hanson Place, 5th Floor
Brooklyn, NY 11217
Phone: 718-783-2000
Fax: 718-783-1593
Website: www.witness.org

Make Poverty History

That pretty much says it all! Our final contribution to this resource guide is an organization that serves as a clearinghouse for the global fight against poverty and misery in all its forms: The One Campaign. From social justice campaigns to freeing prisoners, from updates on the fight against AIDS to attempts to push for fair trade agreements or stop genocide, The One Campaign is the train stop for thousands of nongovernmental organizations around the world who want to put an end to poverty. You can visit the organization's website at www.one.org regularly for updates and insights, or when you're just looking for a fresh place to jump in. The One Campaign website is also where you can cast your vote to add your voice to millions of other world citizens in the fight to end poverty. We hope this guide has been one small encouragement along that journey . . . See you in the trenches.

Discussion Guide

The following are a series of studies for individual or small-group study that we have set up to follow the sections of this book. You can do these studies in six straight weeks (covering two sessions a week), or study the book section by section (which would take you through 11 weeks of study). You may also choose to read through the book as a group, project by project.

If you do these studies in a group session, talk through the introductory material of each section before you go into the Bible study for each. Be sensitive to the needs and interests of your group to know which sections could be touched on more lightly or heavily in your discussions. In addition, each session might be greatly enhanced by a friend, an acquaintance, a member of your church or a guest who can speak from personal experience on one or more of the topics. For example, if the session is on "poverty," try to find someone who has lived in those circumstances, or someone who works with the poor every day.

Whenever possible, this person should be someone known to the group—perhaps someone from your church. This is to prevent the idea from forming in the group members' minds that they are doing things for people "out there"—you want them to be left with the sense that we are all a part of the same Body. The success of this portion of the study is dependent on your ability to find someone who can flesh out the concept for the people in your group. Those in your small group might also be an excellent resource to help you find these presenters and guests. Show them the list of subjects before the first session and ask them to help you find leads.

Each session will have the same basic format and last approximately 50 minutes. Here is our suggestion for how to tackle each Bible study session:

1. Getting Started (5 minutes)
2. Exploring the Word (10 minutes)
3. Special Guest (10 minutes)
4. Reflection on the Christian's Responsibility (10 minutes)
5. Personal Application (5 minutes)
6. Further Action Ideas (5 minutes)
7. Looking Ahead (5 minutes)

The following general guidelines will help you organize and conduct each study session. Keep in mind that the optimum discussion-group size is 10 to 15 people. A smaller group may lose interest unless everyone has a high level of commitment. A larger group will require strong leadership skills to help everyone participate meaningfully.

1. Schedule Meeting Times
If you are leading a group that already meets regularly, such as a church class or a Bible study group, decide how many weeks to spend on this book and schedule your meeting times accordingly.

Consider holidays or other events that might affect continuity of group members' attendance.

2. Recruit a Core Group

If you want to start a new Bible study group or Christian activists group, enlist two or three people as a nucleus for the group. Work with these individuals to determine the meeting time, dates and place that are best for your group and involve them in inviting other people to participate. Your core group members will be instrumental in helping you make follow-up phone calls to the people you invite to remind them of the meeting times and places.

3. Bring the Snacks

Plan to have some light snacks at each session to encourage an atmosphere of friendly conversation and fun. Perhaps each person in the group could take a turn providing snacks for each week of the study.

4. Get the Book

Arrange for informal seating and have copies of the book available for each participant. If each person buys the book themselves, they'll be more likely to commit to following with the study and, just as important, completing some of the projects. At the first meeting, you might briefly share one or two personal ways this book has challenged or motivated you—although this shouldn't be a sales pitch for the book.

5. Be Open and Honest

As the leader, demonstrate honest sharing with your group members and be open with them about your desire to live out your commitment to Christ. Keep in mind that you don't have to be the "expert," even though you are the group leader. The group will appreciate your being a fellow learner as you go through the study.

6. Encourage Sharing

Sharing insights and experiences is a good approach to beginning any of the sessions that follow. As the study progresses and participants become comfortable with one another, open some sessions by inviting participants to share one step they have taken to change the world since the last session.

7. Have a Discussion Time

In each session, lead the participants in discussing the listed questions. If you have more than 8 or 10 people in your group, assign some of the questions to be discussed in smaller groups, and then invite each group to share one or two insights with the larger group. Alternate large-group and small-group discussion times to give variety and to allow every participant a comfortable option in which to contribute. Try various combinations in forming small groups: groups based on Christian service or activism experience, separate groups for males and females, groups based on geographical location within the community, and so on.

8. Guide the Discussion

In guiding the discussions, the following tips might be helpful:

- If a question or comment is raised that is off the subject, either suggest that it be dealt with at another time or ask the group if they would prefer to pursue the new issue at the current time.

- If someone talks too much, direct a few questions specifically to other people, making sure not to put a shy person on the spot. Talk privately with the "dominator," asking for his or her cooperation in helping to draw out a few of the quieter participants.

- If someone does not participate verbally, assign a few questions to be discussed in pairs, trios or other small groups. Or, distribute paper and pencils and ask people to write their answer to a specific question or topic. Then invite several people, including the shy ones, to read what they wrote.

- If someone asks a question and you do not know the answer, admit it and move on. If the question calls for insight about personal experience, invite participants to comment.

- If the question requires specialized knowledge, offer to look up the answer on the Internet or from another source before the next session.

9. Pray
Finally, pray regularly for the sessions and the participants.

Poverty

CARING FOR THE POOR

Biblical Basis: Genesis 41:41-57

Getting Started (5 Minutes)

Begin by asking, "What unique role do the poor play in our society?"

Exploring the Word (10 Minutes)

Overview of Genesis 41:41-57:

    I. Joseph is given charge of Egypt—Genesis 41:41-45

   II. Joseph and Egypt are prosperous—Genesis 41:46-52

  III. Famine in the land—Genesis 41:53-55

  IV. Joseph provides food—Genesis 41:56-57

Ask a group member to read the Scripture passage aloud. As a group, outline the events of this passage. Say, "Through a dream, God told Joseph of the coming famine. What options were there for Egypt's prosperity? What responsibility did Joseph have? And to whom?"

Special Guest (10 Minutes)

Introduce your guest. We suggest you invite someone who has lived in poverty.

Reflection on the Christian's Responsibility (10 Minutes)

Discuss the following questions:

1. In what different ways does poverty express itself today?
2. What do you think are the key causes of poverty?
3. What can be done to rectify these problems?
4. Beyond providing for material needs, how can Christians minister to poor people?

Personal Application (5 Minutes)

Take a few moments of silence to think through some ways God is nudging you to involve your life with poor people. Write them down. Share them with a group member.

Further Action Ideas (5 Minutes)

Consider the projects in the "Poverty" section. As a group, think about how you, your group members and your entire church might minister to poor people.

Looking Ahead (5 Minutes)

Ask group members to read the next section on evangelism before the next session. Close with group prayer for God's movement and your action among poor people.

Evangelism

PROCLAIMING THE GOOD NEWS

Biblical Basis: Jonah 1–4

Getting Started (5 Minutes)

Before the session, record the following portion from the opening passage of this section on a cassette tape or computer:

> A song that some of us might have learned in Sunday School says: "This world is not my home, I'm just a-passin' through. My treasures are laid up, somewhere beyond the blue. The angels beckon me from heaven's open door, and I can't feel at home in this world anymore." A great song, but it is only half true! Christians must live in the tension of *not* being at home while at the same time being at home.
>
> This world is half our home. Christ has put us here for the purpose of planting our roots deep in the soil of contemporary society. By our persistent Spirit-filled living, we enlarge the influence of the Kingdom and demonstrate God's love to the world. Although we are told not to be *of* the world, we are called to live *in* the world. Maybe our traditional evangelistic programs serve as a trade-off: We like the security of the Church, but we feel we ought to do something about the people "out there." So we design ways to temporarily breathe.

Begin the session by playing the tape recording. Ask, "What responses does the tension of not being at home while at the same time being at home elicit in most Christians?"

Exploring the Word (10 Minutes)
Overview of Jonah 1–4:

    I. Jonah is disobedient—Jonah 1:1-11
   II. Jonah is swallowed by the fish—Jonah 1:12–2:10
  III. The Ninevites repent—Jonah 3
  IV. God is compassionate—Jonah 4

Divide members into four groups. Assign one of the four above Scripture passages to each group. Have each group read the passage and summarize Jonah's actions, God's actions and the results. Allow groups to record and share their findings.

Special Guest (10 Minutes)
Introduce your guest. We suggest you invite someone who recently became a Christian.

Reflection on the Christian's Responsibility (10 Minutes)
Discuss the following questions:

1. To what extent are we responsible to and for the unsaved?
2. How do the evangelism efforts that you are aware of convey or not convey the concern God has for the unsaved?
3. How might we be insulating ourselves from those outside the family of faith?

Personal Application (5 Minutes)
Take a few moments of silence to think through some of the ways God is nudging you to move out of your Christian enclave and into the world. Write each of these ways down on a sheet of paper. Share them with a group member.

The Environment
TENDING GOD'S CREATION

Biblical Basis
Genesis 1:26-31; 2:4-15; Leviticus 25:3-12

Getting Started (5 Minutes)
Begin by saying, "Picture a beautiful, scenic location that you have visited. Consider the different elements of this place. What does this scenic location tell you about God?"

Exploring the Word (10 Minutes)
Overview of Genesis 1:26-31; 2:4-15:

    I. God creates us—Genesis 1:26-27; 2:4-7
    II. God's garden described—Genesis 2:8-14
    III. We are given responsibility for the garden—
        Genesis 1:28-31; 2:15

Overview of Leviticus 25:3-12:

    I. Instructions to work the land—Leviticus 25:3
    II. Sabbath year of rest for the land—Leviticus 25:4-7
    III. Year of jubilee for the land—Leviticus 25:8-12

Divide members into two groups. Have one group read Genesis 1:26-31 and 2:4-15 and list God's purpose in creating us and our responsibilities for tending His creation. Have the other group read Leviticus 25:3-12 and list the results of the Sabbath year and year of jubilee on the land. Allow groups to share their findings.

Special Guest (10 Minutes)
Introduce your guest. We suggest you invite a nonprofessional environmentalist.

Reflection on the Christian's Responsibility (10 Minutes)
Discuss the following questions:

1. What impact can Christians and the local church have on environments outside a particular geographical location?
2. How does our call to care for creation coincide with and differ from other environmental movements?
3. Why has the Church been slow in becoming involved in the care of God's creation?

Personal Application (5 Minutes)
Take a few moments of silence to think through some of the ways God is nudging you to be involved with the environment. Write each of these ways down on a sheet of paper. Share them with a group member.

Further Action Ideas (5 Minutes)
Consider the projects in the "Environment" section. As a group, think about how you, your group members and your entire church can be better stewards of God's creation.

Looking Ahead (5 Minutes)
Ask group members to read the next section on prisoners before the next session. Close with group prayer for God's movement and your action in the area of the environment.

Prisoners
BEFRIENDING THE OUTCAST

Biblical Basis
Acts 16:16-40

Getting Started (5 Minutes)
Begin by asking, "What are the titles of some films or books that portray prison life? What do they communicate about prisoners?"

Exploring the Word (10 Minutes)
Overview of Acts 16:16-40:

    I. Claims are made against Paul and Silas—Acts 16:16-21
    II. Paul and Silas are beaten and imprisoned—Acts 16:22-24
    III. An earthquake releases Paul and Silas—Acts 16:25-30
    IV. The jailer and his family are baptized—Acts 16:31-34
    V. Paul requests justice—Acts 16:35-40

Ask a group member to read the Scripture passage aloud. As a group, outline the actions and attitude of the jailer toward Paul and Silas. Ask, "What caused this change in the jailer?"

Special Guest (10 Minutes)
Introduce your guest. We suggest you invite someone who has been imprisoned or who is a family member of such a person.

Reflection on the Christian's Responsibility (10 Minutes)
Discuss the following questions:

1. What challenges are unique to a ministry to prisoners?
2. How can we remove the stigma of having a loved one in prison?
3. What can be done to keep in mind the needs of prisoners who are out of our sight?

Personal Application (5 Minutes)

Take a few moments of silence to think through some ways God is nudging you to be involved with prisoners. Write each of these ways down on a sheet of paper. Share them with a group member.

Further Action Ideas (5 Minutes)

Consider the projects in the "Prisoners" section. As a group, think about how you, your group members and your entire church could minister to prisoners.

Looking Ahead (5 Minutes)

Ask group members to read the next section on the oppressed before the next session. Close with group prayer for God's movement and your action among prisoners.

The Oppressed
UPHOLDING THE DOWNTRODDEN

Biblical Basis
Exodus 1:8-16

Getting Started (5 Minutes)
Begin by having each group member complete the following:
Oppression is . . .

Exploring the Word (10 Minutes)
Overview of Exodus 1:8-16:

    I. The Israelites are oppressed into slavery—Exodus 1:8-11
   II. The oppression is increased—Exodus 1:12-14
  III. The king tries to have Jewish boys killed—Exodus 1:15-16

Have a group member read the Scripture passage aloud. Have group members list the changes that would have occurred in the life (work, family, religious practice and so forth) of the average Israelite as a result of the oppression.

Special Guest (10 Minutes)
Introduce your guest. We suggest that you invite someone who has lived in an oppressive situation.

Reflection on the Christian's Responsibility (10 Minutes)
Discuss the following questions:

   1. What unique role can a Christian who is in an oppressive situation play in bringing about justice?

2. In working toward justice, how should the actions of Christians differ from those of non-Christians?
3. Think of an oppressive situation that is beyond the immediate influence of your group. What action can be taken in this situation?

Personal Application (5 Minutes)

Take a few moments of silence to think through some of the ways God is nudging you to be more involved with oppressed people. Write each of these ways down on a sheet of paper. Share them with a group member.

Further Action Ideas (5 Minutes)

Consider the projects in "The Oppressed" section. As a group, think about how you, your group members and your entire church could minister to oppressed people.

Looking Ahead (5 Minutes)

Ask group members to read the next section on the elderly before the next session. Close with group prayer for God's movement and your action among oppressed people.

The Elderly

HONORING THE WISE

Biblical Basis

Joshua 14:6-14

Getting Started (5 Minutes)

Begin by showing a picture of an elderly person. Say, "What one word comes to mind when you look at this picture?" Have each person respond. Repeat using other pictures.

Exploring the Word (10 Minutes)

Overview of Joshua 14:6-14:

    I. Caleb reminds Joshua of the past—Joshua 14:6-9

    II. Caleb declares his competence—Joshua 14:10-11

    III. Caleb requests his promised land—Joshua 14:12

    IV. Joshua blesses and rewards Caleb—Joshua 14:13-14

Divide group members into pairs. Have each pair read the Scripture passage and write a description (physical, emotional, intellectual) of Caleb. Have group members share their findings.

Special Guest (10 Minutes)

Introduce your guest. We suggest you invite an elderly person from your church or neighborhood.

Reflection on the Christian's Responsibility (10 Minutes)

Discuss the following questions:

1. What are some of the greatest concerns of elderly people?
2. How might we be insulating ourselves from the elderly?
3. What special benefits are there in ministering to the elderly?

Personal Application (5 Minutes)

Take a few moments of silence to think through some of the ways God is nudging you to be involved with elderly people. Write each of these ways down on a sheet of paper. Share them with a group member.

Further Action Ideas (5 Minutes)

Consider the projects in "The Elderly" section. As a group, think about how you, your group members and your entire church could minister to elderly people.

Looking Ahead (5 Minutes)

Ask group members to read the next section on the sick and disabled before the next session. Close with group prayer for God's movement and your action among elderly people.

The Sick and Disabled

SERVING THE AFFLICTED

Biblical Basis
Mark 10:46-52; 2 Samuel 9:1-13

Getting Started (5 Minutes)
Begin by reading from some magazines and/or newspapers on the issue of health care. Ask, "What important issues for a sick or disabled person do these neglect to address?"

Exploring the Word (10 Minutes)
Overview of Mark 10:46-52:

    I. Bartimaeus calls to Jesus—Mark 10:46-47
    II. Jesus responds—Mark 10:48-50
    III. Bartimaeus requests healing—Mark 10:51
    IV. Jesus heals Bartimaeus—Mark 10:52

Overview of 2 Samuel 9:1-13:

    I. David learns of Mephibosheth—2 Samuel 9:1-4
    II. David pledges to care for Mephibosheth—2 Samuel 9:5-8
    III. Ziba is ordered to work for Mephibosheth—2 Samuel 9:9-10
    IV. Mephibosheth lives with David—2 Samuel 9:11-13

Divide members into two groups. Have one group read Mark 10:46-52 and describe how they think Bartimaeus felt at each point in the account. Have the other group read 2 Samuel 9:1-13 and describe what opportunities David provided for Mephibosheth. Bring the group back together and ask members what they think the plight of a sick and disabled person was during Old Testament times.

Special Guest (10 Minutes)

Introduce your guest. We suggest you invite someone who is disabled, has experienced a long-term illness, or is a family member of such a person.

Reflection on the Christian's Responsibility (10 Minutes)

Discuss the following questions:

1. In the past, Christians were leaders in caring for the sick and disabled. What has caused a change in this?
2. What responsibility do we have to the mentally disabled?
3. In what ways do we prevent the disabled from being active participants in our churches?
4. What can Christians do to show God's special love for the sick and disabled?

Personal Application (5 Minutes)

Take a few moments of silence to think through some of the ways God is nudging you to be involved with sick or disabled people. Write each of these ways down on a sheet of paper. Share them with a group member.

Further Action Ideas (5 Minutes)

Consider the projects in "The Sick and Disabled" section. As a group, think about how you, your group members and your entire church could minister to the sick and disabled.

Immigrants

HELPING THOSE NEW TO OUR LAND

Biblical Basis

Matthew 2:13-16

Getting Started (5 Minutes)

Begin by saying, "Imagine that a personal tragedy has forced you to relocate to another country. You don't know the language, people or customs. Your finances are limited, and contact with home is improbable. What will you do?"

Exploring the Word (10 Minutes)

Overview of Matthew 2:13-16:

    I. Joseph is instructed to leave Israel—Matthew 2:13

    II. Joseph, Mary and Jesus flee to Egypt—Matthew 2:14-15

    III. Herod tries to have Jesus killed—Matthew 2:16

Have a group member read aloud the Scripture passage. Say, "Joseph and Mary were Jews who had lived all their lives in Israel. Israel was home to their families and the only land they knew." Ask, "What do you think Mary and Joseph thought and felt as they fled to Egypt? What obstacles did they probably face once they were in Egypt?"

Special Guest (10 Minutes)

Introduce your guest. We suggest you invite someone who has recently arrived in this country.

Reflection on the Christian's Responsibility (10 Minutes)
Discuss the following questions:

1. To what extent are we responsible to and for those who are new to this country?
2. What special efforts can the Body of Christ take to convey God's love for immigrants?
3. How might we be insulating ourselves from immigrants?

Personal Application (5 Minutes)
Take a few moments of silence to think through some ways God is nudging you to be involved with immigrants. Write each of these ways down on a sheet of paper. Share them with a group member.

Further Action Ideas (5 Minutes)
Consider the projects in the "Immigrants" section. As a group, think about how you, your group members and your entire church could minister to immigrants in your area or community.

Looking Ahead (5 Minutes)
Ask group members to read the next section on the world before the next session. Close with group prayer for God's movement and your action among immigrants.

The World

CARING FOR THE PEOPLE OF ALL NATIONS

Biblical Basis

Acts 13:44-48

Getting Started (5 Minutes)

Begin by saying, "Do you agree or disagree that we are to minister first to those who are around us?" Have group members explain why they agree or disagree.

Exploring the Word (10 Minutes)

Overview of Acts 13:44-48:

    I. The Jews speak against Paul and Barnabas—Acts 13:44-45
   II. The gospel is made available to the Gentiles—Acts 13: 46-47
  III. The Gentiles respond—Acts 13:48

Read the passage aloud. Say, "God planned for the message of salvation to spread to the ends of the earth." Ask, "How did this affect the Jews? How did this affect the Gentiles?"

Special Guest (10 Minutes)

Introduce your guest. We suggest that you invite someone who became a Christian as a result of missions work done in the community or overseas.

Reflection on the Christian's Responsibility (10 Minutes)

Discuss the following questions:

1. What has been the Church's response to the spread of other religions around the world, especially Islam?
2. What are the obstacles that keep people from being involved in action, service and evangelism around the world?
3. What impact do overseas evangelism, Christian service and Christians helping to fight diseases such as AIDS around the world have on the local Church body?

Personal Application (5 Minutes)

Take a few moments of silence to think through some of the ways God is nudging you to minister to the poor, sick and oppressed in the world. Write each of these ways down on a sheet of paper. Share them with a group member.

Further Action Ideas (5 Minutes)

Consider the projects in "The World" section. As a group, think about how you, your group members and your entire church could be a better witness to the world.

Looking Ahead (5 Minutes)

Ask group members to read the next section on taking action before the next session. Close with group prayer for God's movement and your action in the area of caring for the people of all nations in the world.

Take Action
IDEAS FOR HEALTHY ACTIVISM

Biblical Basis:
1 Samuel 3:1-18

Getting Started (5 Minutes)
Begin by dividing your group into pairs. Ask, "What current political or social issues are most important to you? In what ways would you change the current political or social climate?"

Exploring the Word (10 Minutes)
Overview of 1 Samuel 3:1-18:

    I. Samuel ministers in the Temple—1 Samuel 3:1-2
    II. God calls Samuel—1 Samuel 3:3-8
    III. Eli instructs Samuel—1 Samuel 3:9
    IV. Samuel listens to God—1 Samuel 3:10-14
    V. Samuel delivers God's message—1 Samuel 3:15-18

Divide group members into pairs and have each pair read the Scripture passage. Ask, "How did God work through Samuel? What caused Samuel to listen to God? When Samuel took action and responded to the Lord, whom did the message influence?" As a group, list the ways that you can influence the people around you through your actions.

Special Guest (10 Minutes)
Introduce your guest. We suggest that you invite a local activist from your church, community or school.

Reflection on the Christian's Responsibility (10 Minutes)

Discuss the following questions:

1. What special challenges do the issues prevalent today bring to the Body of Christ?
2. What can we do to meet these challenges?
3. How would those particular actions demonstrate the love of Jesus Christ to our culture?
4. Do the actions of Christians today demonstrate the love of Christ? How could those actions be shifted to more fully demonstrate Christ's love?

Personal Application (5 Minutes)

Take a few moments of silence to think through some of the ways God is nudging you to involve yourself in healthy activism or some form of political or social involvement. Write each of these ways down on a sheet of paper. Share them with a group member.

Further Action Ideas (5 Minutes)

Consider the projects in the "Take Action" section. As a group, think about how you, your group members and your entire church could be activists for a major political or social issue.

Looking Ahead (5 Minutes)

Ask group members to read the final project before the next session. Close with group prayer for God's movement through your actions in the community and the world.

A Final Project

MAKE POVERTY HISTORY

Biblical Basis
Matthew 11:16-19; John 10:10

Getting Started (5 Minutes)
The Final Project is all about celebrating life and ministering to the poor, the oppressed, the prisoner, the elderly, the sick, the disabled, the immigrant and others around the world who are suffering. Begin by dividing group members into pairs. Ask the group to share their most rewarding experience in terms of helping others or helping to make a difference in the world.

Exploring the Word (10 Minutes)
Overview of Matthew 11:16-19:

    I. Jesus assesses the people—Matthew 11:16
   II. The people reject every approach—Matthew 11:17
  III. Jesus chooses life—Matthew 11:18-19

Ask a group member to read the Scripture passage aloud. Say, "In the same way that John the Baptist's approach was appropriate for his ministry, Jesus' approach fulfilled the needs of those around Him." Ask, "What excuses did people use for rejecting Jesus' approach?" Ask a group member to read John 10:10 aloud. Ask, "What does 'to the full' or 'abundantly' mean?"

Special Guest (10 Minutes)
Introduce your guest. We suggest you invite someone who is involved in a healthy, life-promoting Christian ministry in your area.

Reflections on the Christian's Responsibility (10 Minutes)

Discuss the following questions:

1. What are the most neglected aspects in celebrating and promoting life in your church?
2. What attitudes or patterns of behavior keep Christians from being completely pro-life?
3. In what ways can Christians be the leaders in living life to the fullest?

Personal Application (5 Minutes)

Take a few moments of silence to think through some of the ways God is nudging you to get more involved in your community—especially in projects that involve the celebration of life. Write each of these ways down on a sheet of paper. Share them with a group member.

Further Action Ideas (5 Minutes)

Consider the final project this section. As a group, think about how you, your group members and your entire church could celebrate and promote life by getting involved with The One Campaign or other similar ministries on a regional level.

Endnotes

Section 1—Poverty: Caring for the Poor

1. "Progress Toward the Millennium Development Goals, 1990-2005," United Nations Statistics Division, June 13, 2005. http://millenniumindi cators.un.org/unsd/mi/mi_coverfinal.htm (accessed June 2006). Statistics compiled by an inter-agency technical group of the United Nations system and Organization for Economic Co-operation and Development, led by the Statistics Division, Department of Economic and Social Affairs of the United Nations Secretariat.
2. According to the International Programs Center of the U.S. Census Bureau, the estimated world population as of January 1, 2006, was 6,488,578,564. http://www.census.gov/ipc/www/popclockworld.html (accessed June 2006).
3. The New York City Coalition Against Hunger home page. http://www.nyc cah.org/ (accessed June 2006).
4. "World Hunger: Overview of the Current Situation," Rainbow World Fund. http://www.rainbowfund.org/hunger/ (accessed June 2006).
5. Data from "The State of Food Insecurity in the World" report of the Food and Agriculture Organization of the United Nations, cited at Erwin Northoff, "Hunger Slows Progress Toward Millennium Development Goals," The Food and Agriculture Organization Newsroom, November 22, 2005. http://www. fao.org/newsroom/en/news/2005/1000151/index.html (accessed June 2006).
6. Mark Nord, M. Andrews and S. Carlson, "Household Food Security in the United States, 2004," United States Department of Agriculture and Economic Research Service, cited at "Child Hunger Facts," America's Second Harvest. http://www.secondharvest.org/learn_about_hunger/child_ hunger_facts.html (accessed June 2006).
7. "World Development Indicators 2005," World Bank Study, cited at "20 Questions About Poverty and Development," The World Bank. http://www1. worldbank.org/prem/poverty/quiz/whole.htm (accessed June 2006).
8. Data from the "Current Population Survey, 2005 Annual Social and Economic Supplement," sample survey of approximately 100,000 U.S. households nationwide. Cited at "Poverty: 2004 Highlights," U.S. Census Bureau, Housing and Household Economic Statistics Division, August 30, 2005. http://www.census.gov/hhes/www/poverty/poverty04/pov04hi.html (accessed June 2006).

Section 2—Evangelism: Proclaiming the Good News

1. William Walker, "This World Is Not My Home," 1875, quoted at Christian Classics Ethereal Library. http://www.ccel.org/s/southern_harmony/ sharm/sharm/gif/t=This+World+is+Not+My+Home/520.html (accessed June 2006).

2. Study conducted by the Evangelical Fellowship of Canada, cited by Kathryn Mulolani in "Everyone Benefits from Short-Term Missions," Canada's Christian Community Online, October 2003. http://www.chris tianity.ca/mission/global/2004/05.001.html.

3. "The State of World Evangelism," *Mission Frontiers: The Bulletin of the U.S. Center for World Mission*. http://www.missionfrontiers.org/newslinks/statewe.htm (accessed June 2006). According to this site, of the 410,000 missionaries from all branches of Christendom, only 2 to 3 percent work among unreached people groups.

Section 3: The Environment: Tending God's Creation

1. Maltbie D. Babcock, "This Is My Father's World," 1901, quoted at the cyber-hymnal. http://www.cyberhymnal.org/htm/t/i/tismyfw.htm (accessed May 2006).

2. Chris Isidore, "Exxon Mobil Sets Profit Record: Nation's No. 1 Oil Company Reports Larger Than Expected Jump in 4Q Income to Cap Record Year," CNNMoney.com, January 20, 2006. http://money.cnn.com/2006/01/30/news/companies/exxon_earns/ (accessed May 2006).

3. Jeffrey Ball, "Exxon Chief Makes a Cold Calculation on Global Warming," *Wall Street Journal*, June 15, 2005.

4. "Compact Fluorescent Light Bulb Factsheet," Earth Day Network. http://www.earthday.net/resources/2006materials/cf-facts.aspx (accessed June 2006). See also "CFL Compact Fluorescent Light Bulbs" at http://www.cflbulbs.com.

5. The International Union for the Conservation of Nature and Natural Resources Red List for 2006 contains 16,119 species threatened with extinction. Note that this figure is an underestimate of the total number of threatened species, as it is based on an assessment of less than 3 percent of the world's 1.9 million species. http://www.iucn.org/themes/ssc/red_list_2004/GSAexecsumm_EN.htm (accessed June 2006).

6. Alice Horrigan and Jim Motavalli, "Talking Trash: Recycling Under Attack," *Emagazine.com*. http://www.emagazine.com/view/?409 (accessed June 2006).

7. "Flags at Central Valley Schools Signal Air Quality," *Breath Matters* Monthly E-Newsletter, The American Lung Association of California. http://www.californialung.org/ALAC/enews0505.html (accessed June 2006).

8. The United States Department of Agriculture and Animal Welfare Enforcement 2001 report stated that 1,236,903 animals were used in experiments by registered research facilities in the United States. The data did not include mice and rats, which estimates suggest represent about 10 percent of the animals used in experiments. http://www.kids4research.org/animals.html (accessed June 2006). Worldwide estimates suggest that 100 million to 200 million animals are used in experiments each year. http://en.wikipedia.org/wiki/Animal_testing#United_States (accessed June 2006).

9. In 2006, enrollment for Arizona State University surpassed that of all other universities when measured by the number of full-time undergraduate students enrolled.

10. Rhett A. Butler, "A World Imperiled: Forces Behind Forest Loss," Mongabay .com, January 9, 2006. http://rainforests.mongabay.com/0801.htm (accessed June 2006). The Food and Agriculture Organization of the United Nations estimates that 10.4 million hectares of tropical forest were permanently destroyed each year in the period from 2000 to 2005, an increase since the 1990 to 2000 period, when around 10.16 million hectares of forest were lost. Among primary forests, annual deforestation rose to 6.26 million hectares from 5.41 million hectares in the same period.

11. "Rainforest Facts," Rainforest Foundation U.S. http://www.rainforestfoun dation.org/library.php (accessed July 2006). According to this website, approximately 50 million indigenous people depend directly on tropical forests for shelter and food. An additional 2.5 million people live in cleared areas adjacent to the forests and also depend on them for various resources.

Section 4—Prisoners: Befriending the Outcast

1. U.S. Bureau of Justice statistics (December 31, 2004), cited at "Prison Population Totals," The International Centre for Prison Studies (King's College, London, England). http://www.prisonstudies.org/ (accessed June 2006). China had the second highest number of incarcerations at 1,548,498 (National Prison Administration, December 2003); Russia was third at 847,000 (National Prison Administration, January 4, 2006).

2. Roy Walmsley, *World Prison Population List, 3rd ed.* (London, UK: Home Office Research, Development and Statistics Directorate, 2002), p. 1. Online version available at http://www.homeoffice.gov.uk/rds/pdfs/r166.pdf (accessed June 2006).

3. Allen J. Beck, Ph.D., Jennifer Karberg and Paige M. Harrison, "Bureau of Justice Statistics, Prison and Jail Inmates at Midyear 2001" (Washington, DC: US Dept. of Justice, April 2002), pp. 1, 12, table 15. The rate of incarceration for African-American women was 380 per 100,000; for Hispanic women, 119 per 100,000; for white women, 67 per 100,000; for Hispanic men, 1,668 per 100,000.

4. U.S. Census Bureau, data for 2000, cited at "Incarcerated America: Human Rights Watch Backgrounder," Human Rights Watch, April 2003. http://www.hrw.org/backgrounder/usa/incarceration/ (accessed June 2006).

5. "Amnesty International: History," Wikipedia.com. http://en.wikipedia.org/wiki/Amnesty_International#History (accessed June 2006). Amnesty International was officially founded in 1961 by Peter Benenson, the British lawyer, and his colleague, Eric Baker. The Amnesty International logo was created in 1962 by Diana Redhouse, who designed the image based on the old Chinese proverb, "Better to light a candle than curse the darkness."

6. "Tools for Citizens: Tips and Ideas for Enhancing Your Political Voice," 20/20 Vision. http://www.2020vision.org/resources/r_activists.htm#writ ingletters (accessed June 2006).

Section 5—The Oppressed: Upholding the Downtrodden

1. Francis Cruz, "Tunnel of Oppression Still Shocking," *The New Paltz Oracle,* November 3, 2005, vol. 77, issue 7. http://www.newpaltz.edu/oracle/arti cle.cfm?id=2055 (accessed June 2006).

2. The word "genocide" was coined by Polish-born U.S. jurist Raphael Lemkin in his 1944 work, *Axis Rule in Occupied Europe,* to describe the extermination of the Jewish race under the Nazi regime (Greek *genos,* "race or kind," Latin *cide,* "to kill"). http://www.etymonline.com/index.php?term=genocide (accessed June 2006).

3. "New Analysis Claims Darfur Deaths Near 400,000," Coalition for International Justice press release, April 21, 2005. http://www.cij.org/ index.cfm?fuseaction=homepage (accessed June 2006). Accurate numbers of the deaths that have occurred in the conflict in Darfur have been difficult to obtain due to the Sudanese government censorship of foreign journalists. Estimates of the deaths range from 50,000 (World Health Organization, September 2004) to 450,000 (Dr. Eric Reeves, April 2006). Most humanitarian groups use the figure of 400,000 proposed by the Coalition for International Justice. See "Darfur Conflict," Wikipedia.com. http://en.wikipedia.org/wiki/Darfur_conflict#_note-New_analysis_claims_Darfur_deaths_near_400.2C000 (accessed June 2006).

4. "Little Boy and Fat Man," National Atomic Museum. http://www.atomic museum.com/tour/dd2.cfm (accessed June 2006).

5. Mary Kimani, "The Media Trial Accounting for the Rwandan Genocide— Impressions of the 'Media Trial,'" Internews Network Report from the International Criminal Tribunal for Rwanda, *ITCR Reports,* December 5, 2000. http://www.internews.org/activities/ICTR_reports/ICTRmedia_12_00.htm (accessed June 2006). It is estimated that 800,000 Rwandan Tutsis and moderate Hutus were killed within the space of 100 days, making this the fastest and most encompassing genocide known to mankind.

6. "A Summary of United Nations Agreements on Human Rights," The United Nations, January 25, 1997. http://www.hrweb.org/legal/undocs.html (accessed June 2006). On December 9, 1948, the United Nations General Assembly unanimously adopted the Genocide Convention, and by October 16, 1950, 20 countries had ratified the convention. However, the United States refused to ratify the convention on the grounds that it might be unfairly used to target American citizens. The Senate finally ratified the convention in 1986, 40 years after it was first drafted, with numerous revisions and caveats. It officially became U.S. law in November 1988. See "The Genocide Convention,"

CBC News online, September 20, 2004. http://www.cbc.ca/news/background/sudan/genocide_convention.html (accessed June 2006).

7. "Bosnian Rape Camp Trial Opens," BBC News, March 20, 2000. http://news.bbc.co.uk/1/hi/world/europe/683846.stm. In 1993, a European Community commission estimated that there were 20,000 rape victims in the conflict, but a study by the Bosnian government put the figure at 50,000. Today, commissions such as the International Criminal Court are formally trying soldiers who participate in such gang rapes.

8. "Our Mission," Women in Black, November 11, 2002. http://www.womeninblack.net/mission.html (accessed June 2006).

9. "Women in Black Vigils," Women in Black. http://www.womeninblack.org/about.html (accessed June 2006).

10. You can find the Universal Declaration of Human Rights on the United Nations' website at www.un.org/Overview/rights.html.

11. According to Family Safe Media, in 2005, U.S. porn revenue was $12 billion ($57 billion worldwide), a figure that exceeded the combined revenues of ABC, CBS and NBC. See "Pornography Statistics," Family Safe Media. http://www.familysafemedia.com/pornography_statistics.html (accessed June 2006).

12. "The Human Right to Adequate Housing Fact Sheet No. 21," Office of the High Commissioner for Human Rights, United Nations. http://193.194.138.190/html/menu6/2/fs21.htm (accessed June 2006).

13. "Jimmy Carter and Habitat for Humanity: Worldwide View Shared by Carter and Habitat," Habitat for Humanity. http://www.habitat.org/how/carter.aspx (accessed June 2006).

14. Patricia Tjaden and Nancy Thoennes, "Extent, Nature, and Consequences of Intimate Partner Violence," The National Institute of Justice and the Centers for Disease Control and Prevention, July 2000. Data based on the National Violence Against Women Survey conducted from November 1995 to May 1996. Online version available at http://www.ncjrs.gov/txtfiles1/nij/181867.txt (accessed June 2006).

15. "Trafficking in Human Beings," Wikipedia.com. http://en.wikipedia.org/wiki/Human_trafficking#Extent (accessed June 2006). A U.S. Government report published in 2003 estimates that between 800,000 to 900,000 people are trafficked across international borders each year, with the greatest number being in South East Asia, Japan, Russia and Europe (this figure does include those who are trafficked solely within a particular country). Between 20,000 and 40,000 are trafficked into the United States each year.

Section 7—The Sick and Disabled: Serving the Afflicted

1. "2006 Report on the Global Aids Epidemic, Annex 2: HIV Estimates and Data, 2005 and 2003." http://www.unaids.org/en/HIV_data/2006GlobalReport/default.asp (accessed June 2006).

2. "Goal: Combat HIV/AIDS, Malaria and Other Diseases," Unicef. http://www.unicef.org/mdg/disease.html (accessed June 2006).

3. For a current version of the American Disabilities Act Guidelines for Buildings and Facilities, visit the United States Access Board at http://www.access-board.gov/adaag/html/adaag.htm.

4. Gregg Piburn, *Beyond Chaos: One Man's Journey Alongside His Chronically Ill Wife* (Atlanta, GA: Arthritis Foundation, 1999), n.p. http://www.findarti cles.com/p/articles/mi_m0ISW/is_2002_Dec/ai_94538663 (accessed June 2006).

5. Peter T. Kilborn, "Disabled Spouses Are Increasingly Forced to Go It Alone," *New York Times,* May 31, 1999. http://query.nytimes.com/gst/fullpage.html? sec=health&res=9F07E0DD1230F932A05756C0A96F958260 (accessed July 2006).

6. Maha Al-Azar, "At Labor Department, Enabling the Enabled; Assistant Secretary Can Relate to Those He's Trying to Aid," U.S. Department of Labor, October 27, 2003. http://www.dol.gov/odep/media/post.htm (accessed June 2006). According to the U.S. Census Bureau, the current disabled unemployed population includes approximately 53 million people.

7. David Hughes, "Advocates Work to Boost Unemployment of the Disabled," *The Atlanta Journal-Constitution,* 2006. http://jobnews.ajcjobs.com/news/con tent/careercenter/articles/2006_0507_diverse1.html (accessed June 2006).

Section 8—Immigrants: Helping Those New to Our Land

1. Kelly Jefferys and Nancy Rytina, "U.S. Permanent Residents: 2005," U.S. Department of Homeland Security Office of Immigration Statistics, April 2006, Table 3. Of the 1,122,373 total number of green cards issued in 2005, 161,445 went to natives of Mexico, 84,681 went to natives of India, and 69,967 went to natives of China.

2. "Record number of Indian nationals received green cards in 2005: CSIS," *DNA World,* June 11, 2006. http://www.dnaindia.com/report.asp?NewsID= 1034915 (accessed June 2006). "Under the employment category, India again claimed the largest number of green cards last year due to the large number of software professionals who had migrated to the United States in search of jobs in the 90s."

3. Jennifer Van Hook, Frank D. Bean and Jeffrey Passel, "Unauthorized Migrants Living in the United States: A Mid-Decade Portrait," Migration Information Source, September 1, 2005. http://www.migrationinformation.org/ Feature/display.cfm?ID=329 (accessed June 2006). According to recent surveys, in 2004, 35.7 million people in the United States were foreign born (approximately 12 percent of the U.S. population), and approximately 10.3 million people in this group were unauthorized immigrants. Nearly 6 million of all unauthorized immigrants were born in Mexico; 2.5 million were born in Central and South America; 1 million were from countries in

Asia; 600,000 were from Europe; and 400,000 were from Africa.

4. "More Immigrants Take to Streets to Protest Proposed Laws," *Fox News*, April 11, 2006. http://www.foxnews.com/story/0,2933,191142,00.html (accessed June 2006). Rallies during the month of April were held in 10 states and included crowds of up to 500,000 in Dallas, Texas; 100,000 in Phoenix, Arizona; 50,000 in San Diego, California; and 20,000 in Salt Lake City, Utah. Dozens of rallies and student walkouts were also held in cities around the country including Los Angeles, Chicago and New York.

5. United Nations High Commissioner for Refugees data, quoted at "Frequently Asked Questions," Department of Health and Human Services Centers for Disease Control and Prevention. http://www.cdc.gov/nceh/ierh/FAQ.htm (accessed June 2006).

6. Charles Tilly, "Violence, Terror and Politics as Usual," *Boston Review*, Summer 2002. http://www.bostonreview.net/BR27.3/tilly.html#1 (accessed June 2006).

Section 9—The World: Caring for the People of All Nations

1. "The History of the Red Cross," American Red Cross. http://www.seattleredcross.org/aboutus/history/index.htm (accessed June 2006). The American Red Cross was founded by Clara Barton, a schoolteacher, in 1881 and officially sanctioned by the United States in 1882.

2. Lee Jong-Wook and Carol Bellamy, "Meeting the MDG Drinking-water and Sanitation Target: A Mid-term Assessment of Progress," World Health Organization. http://www.who.int/water_sanitation_health/monitoring/jmp2004/en/.

3. "Millennium Development Goals," United Nations, 2005. http://www.un.org/millenniumgoals/# (accessed June 2006).

4. "Truth and Reconciliation Commission," Wikipedia.org. http://en.wikipedia.org/wiki/Truth_and_Reconciliation_Commission (accessed June 2006). For an online version of the Truth and Reconciliation Commission of South Africa Report, March 21, 2003, go to http://www.info.gov.za/otherdocs/2003/trc/.

5. "Amnesty Hearings and Decisions: Summary of Amnesty Decisions," Truth and Reconciliation Committee, January 11, 2000. http://www.doj.gov.za/trc/ trc_frameset.htm (accessed June 2006).

6. "History of South Africa in the Apartheid Era: Creation of Apartheid," Wikipedia.com. http://en.wikipedia.org/wiki/Apartheid (accessed June 2006).

7. "Prejudice and Discrimination: Apartheid Case Study," Re:Quest Website for Teaching About Christianity in Religious Education. http://www.request.org.uk/issues/topics/prejudice/prejudice09.htm (accessed June 2006).

8. "Support Process," Evangelical Free Church of America. http://www.efca.org/international/giving/supportprocess.html (accessed June 2006).

Endnotes

Section 10—Take Action: Ideas for Healthy Activism

1. Christian Peacemaker Teams homepage, http://www.cpt.org/ (accessed June 2006).

2. "Major Religious Groups," Wikipedia.com. http://en.wikipedia.org/wiki/Major_world_religions (accessed June 2006).

3. Data from International Institute for Strategic Studies, U. S. Department of Defense, cited by Anup Shah, "In Context: U.S. Military Spending Versus Rest of the World," Global Issues, March 27, 2006. http://www.global issues.org/Geopolitics/ArmsTrade/Spending.asp#WorldMilitarySpending (accessed June 2006). According to the data the top 10 spenders include: the United States, $420.7 billion (43% of total); China, $62.5 billion (6%); Russia, $61.9 billion (6%); United Kingdom, $51.1 billion (5%); Japan, $44.7 billion (4%); France, $41.6 billion (4%); Germany, $30.2 billion (3%); India, $22 billion (2%); Saudi Arabia, $21.3 billion (2%); South Korea, 20.7 billion (2%).

4. Robert Drefuss, "The Pentagon's New Spies," Rolling Stone, April 16, 2006. http://www.rollingstone.com/politics/story/9962459/the_pentagons_new_spies (accessed June 2006).

5. "Raging Grannies," Wikipedia.org. http://en.wikipedia.org/wiki/Raging_Grannies (accessed June 2006).

6. Raging Grannies website, www.raginggrannies.com, quoted in Alison Acker and Betty Brightwell, Off Our Rockers and into Trouble: The Raging Grannies (Vancouver, Canada: Heritage House Press, 2004). http://www.heritage house.ca/press_releases/offrockers_press.htm (accessed June 2006).